Working th

An indispensable guide for every woman who wants or needs to work through her pregnancy, offering sound advice on physical, practical and emotional issues, to help get the balance right.

In the same series
COMING LATE TO MOTHERHOOD
  Joan Michelson and Sue Gee
CYSTITIS
  Dr Caroline Shreeve
THE FERTILITY AWARENESS WORKBOOK
  Barbara Kass-Annese and Dr Hal Danzer
THE PREMENSTRUAL SYNDROME
  Dr Caroline Shreeve
THE SECOND NINE MONTHS
  Judith Gansberg and Arthur Mostel
SEX DURING PREGNANCY AND AFTER CHILDBIRTH
  Sylvia Close
THE SINGLE WOMAN'S SURVIVAL GUIDE
  Lee Rodwell
WOMEN ON HYSTERECTOMY
  Nikki Henriques and Anne Dickson
WOMEN ON RAPE
  Jane Dowdeswell
THE WORKING WOMAN'S GUIDE
  Liz Hodgkinson

Working through your pregnancy

How to balance health, happiness and fulfilment

Lee Rodwell

Cartoons by Kate Taylor
Illustrations by Vincent Driver

THORSONS PUBLISHING GROUP
Wellingborough, Northamptonshire
•
Rochester, Vermont

First published 1987

© LEE RODWELL 1987

All rights reserved. No part of this book may be reproduced or utilized in any form or by any means, electronic or mechanical, including photocopying, recording or by any information storage and retrieval system, without permission in writing from the Publisher.

British Library Cataloguing in Publication Data

Rodwell, Lee
Working through your pregnancy.
1. Pregnant women—Employment
I. Title
331.4   HD6053

ISBN 0-7225-1234-1

Printed and bound in Great Britain

Contents

		Page
	Introduction	7
Chapter		
1.	Is it safe to work?	15
2.	Your rights	30
3.	Early days	45
4.	The new you	61
5.	Getting the balance right	74
6.	Other people	98
7.	At home	117
8.	Ante-natal classes	133
9.	A second baby	149
10.	Back to work – or not?	167
	Useful books and information	183
	Index	187

Dedication

For my daughter Tamsin and my son Guy

Introduction

I worked through both my pregnancies. During the first, in 1981, I was a feature writer on the staff of a Fleet Street paper. It was a hot summer that year and, although we worked a four-day week, the hours were long. Travelling to and from work, often on a crowded London tube train, did little to make life easier, particularly during the later stages when I felt, and probably looked, like a pregnant whale!

Despite the discomforts, I have happy memories of those months. I did not suffer from sickness in the early days and I was fit and well in the middle months. In fact I flew off to the Isle of Man when I was seventeen weeks pregnant to cover a story about motor-bike racing, with a photographer who was far more nervous about my condition than I was! Although my bosses did not send me on overnight assignments in the last few weeks, I was by no means desk-bound.

If we had not been in the process of moving house I might well have been tempted to stay on for longer than the thirty-six weeks I did work. As it was, those last four weeks were hardly a restful time. The baby's EDD (estimated date of delivery) and the day set for the actual move were one and the same. In the event, my daughter decided to arrive two days early (neatly letting me out of the hassles of removal men and so on) and she weighed in at a perfectly respectable 6 pounds 14 ounces.

Like any new mother, I was both delighted and relieved that everything had gone well. I was particularly pleased because my obstetrician had suggested several times that I should consider stopping work earlier than I had done, although he had never given any specific reason for this. My editor never put me under any pressure to leave. Other female journalists had worked right up until the day they went into labour so I was not setting any precedents, but in the latter stages of my pregnancy some of my male colleagues had begun to treat me rather like a time bomb that might go off at any minute, which was somewhat unnerving.

Family and close friends were supportive and matter-of-fact about the whole thing, but some of the people I was sent to interview did a double-take when they saw the bump and most of the other women at my ante-natal classes, all of whom stopped work long before I did, either thought I was made of sterling stuff or that I was completely batty.

I worked even longer into my second pregnancy two years later, typing the final chapter of my first book only nine days before my son was born. (I would have had two weeks' grace, but he arrived five days early.) This time the labour was even shorter (fifty-five minutes!) and easier if having a baby in an ambulance can be said to be easy. The baby was a fine, healthy specimen, too, all 8 pounds 6 ounces of him.

By this time, my circumstances had changed. I had left my staff job to freelance and had set up an office at home. In many ways it was easier to work through pregnancy under these conditions. If I had to travel, I could arrange to do so out of the rush hour. I could nap in the comfort of my own bed if I needed to after lunch, and I could pace myself according to my own schedule rather than that of one newspaper.

On the other hand, like many second-time-round mums, I had the demands of a toddler to meet. Of course, I had someone to care for her while I was working, and I have to say that Jan, my nanny, did far more for me in terms of housework while I was pregnant than she would ordinarily have expected to do. In the evenings and at weekends, though, there was no question of putting my feet up or having a lie-in as I had done the time before.

In addition, there were other stresses, mostly financial. Freelances do not get maternity pay, paid sick leave, or paid holidays. No work, no pay - it's that simple. I have no doubt that we could have managed on one salary, as thousands of couples do, but it would have meant a dramatic change in our standard of living. We would certainly have had to sell the house we had bought two years before and probably the car too. As a result I worried about money. I set myself monthly targets and sometimes the pressure to meet these was quite intense.

Deadlines were nothing new to me as a journalist, but I had also set myself the biggest deadline of my life. I was already three months pregnant when I signed the contract to write my first book. Knowing that work would be virtually impossible immediately after the birth, I had agreed to finish the manuscript by the end of May. It was then December and the baby was due at the beginning of June.

Towards the end of the pregnancy there were days when the last thing I wanted to do was sit down and type another few thousand words, but I had no choice. I often sent up a few silent prayers that the baby would not decide to arrive much before schedule.

I also felt rather guilty that I seemed to have little time to think about or plan for the new baby. First time round, even though I had been working, I had always been very conscious of the new life growing inside me. I had taken time to shop for clothes, and buy things for the nursery. This time I left it to Jan to sort out the baby clothes, get out the cot, and dust down the pram.

I kept very quiet about my work at the ante-natal clinic, just in case they should tell me to ease up a little. I let them assume I was 'just a housewife' although it has always seemed to me that being 'just a housewife' is far more physically demanding than many office jobs! And once again I was lucky to have no complications. My blood pressure went up a little at one point but soon sorted itself out and they did nag me about my weight, but that was all. (I have to admit it was far easier to nibble throughout the day at home than it was in the office.) Yet even though I had successfully worked through one pregnancy and produced a healthy baby, I still worried about whether I was really giving this new baby the best start in life.

The reference books I had on pregnancy were not much help either. Some, like my favourite, *Pregnancy and Childbirth* by Sheila Kitzinger, (Michael Joseph, 1980) mention work only in passing, in phrases such as 'if you have recently given up work'.

The Complete Handbook of Pregnancy (Consultant Editor: Wendy Rose-Neil, Sphere, 1984) was rather too blithely reassuring, dismissing the matter in a few sentences and one picture of what appeared to be a female architect or engineer on site.

> Today's mother has a healthy attitude to her pregnancy – she regards it as a perfectly normal stage in womanhood, not as an illness, and she expects others to share that view. Provided her doctor raises no

objections, she can continue working until the last few weeks before the baby is due.

The caption under the picture read: 'Making sure your boss and others at work know you are pregnant should enable you to modify some of your tasks and get extra help with others.'

Consultant obstetrician and gynacologist Gordon Bourne, in his book *Pregnancy* (Pan, 1984) which many women think of as the pregnancy Bible) was as usual thorough, if rather old-fashioned and not particularly reassuring.

> Whether you work during pregnancy depends on individual circumstances and no generalization is possible but certain basic rules can be laid down.
>
> Providing pregnancy is normal there is no reason why a woman should not do reasonable work, on condition that it does not expose her to any risk of accident or undue tiredness. Most women are much happier, especially during their first pregnancy, if they continue with their job than they would be if they sat at home being generally bored. The money is probably important anyway. *Women who already have children have a full-time job on their hands coping with the house and the children as well as with the new pregnancy.* If there is any question or doubt in your mind you should discuss the whole question of work with your doctor or with the doctor at the hospital.
>
> Even in a normal pregnancy it is not usually recommended to continue working after the end of the twenty-ninth week. A lot of women argue, however that they have a sedentary occupation two minutes' walk from home and might just as well go there and bash at the typewriter as stay at home and scrub the floor. Providing they are happy, have sufficient rest, are not becoming overtired and the pregnancy is normal there is no reason why *younger* women should not continue a sedentary job, particularly in their first pregnancy and especially if they do not have far to travel.
>
> Each individual must, however be judged on her merits and a compromise, such as part-time work, may be reached. (My italics)

Advice such as this, however well-meaning, can raise more questions than it answers. What exactly does the Handbook mean by 'the last few weeks'? Does it mean the same as Gordon Bourne's 'not usually recommended to continue working after the end of the twenty-ninth week'? What does Bourne mean by 'risk of accident', and when does tiredness become 'undue tiredness'? What is a younger mother? Someone who is under forty, under thirty-five, under thirty? And is he *really* saying that pregnant women with young children at home should not take on paid work as well, or does he simply mean that mothers should not go back to work?

Just as Bourne seems out of touch with the real anxieties facing women who want to work – or who have to work – and have babies, so does *The Complete Handbook of Pregnancy*. It is all very well to suggest that when you break the news of your soon-to-be happy event, you will instantly find your boss and your workmates rallying round to make life that much easier for you. It does not always happen that way.

One specialist who seems more attuned to the real world than most is Professor Geoffrey Chamberlain, chairman of the department of Obstetrics and Gynaecology at St George's Medical School. In his book, *The Pregnancy Survival Manual,* (Macdonald, 1984) he acknowledges that many women have dual responsibilities for work within the home and formal paid employment outside it. He goes on to point out that once you are pregnant, these responsibilities can become a burden and he also discusses the effects work may have on the unborn child. But he does present a balanced picture.

> All work requires effort and it is probable that the more fatiguing jobs can have some effect on your unborn child. Hard physical work can be associated with a higher incidence of early pre-term labour and smaller babies. If you work is outside the home even getting to work can be a problem. Public transport, with its smoky, tiring and stressful atmosphere, is not the best place for women to be in early pregnancy and taking your own transport can be even more stressful.
>
> However, it would be quite wrong to suggest that, ideally, a pregnant women should abandon her job and devote herself to contemplation of her expanding body. *Boredom and frustration can have just as harmful effects as over-exertion.* (My italics)

He goes on:

> The whole problem of work in pregnancy is a difficult one. If the work you do is not fatiguing, does not involve hazardous chemicals or radiation, and you are used to it, then it is probably wise to continue. You will be bored sitting at home doing nothing and work can be a stimulating place. If, however, your work is fatiguing or the effort of getting to work is overtiring, you should seriously consider giving it up.

There are no hard and fast rules about this except for those in jobs that involve specific chemical or physical hazards. There are many issues to consider and you must decide what will be right in your particular circumstances.

Today, more and more women are having to make this decision. More women work during pregnancy than did thirty years ago, and a larger proportion of women work right up until the last few weeks.

A survey carried out in 1946 showed that 28 per cent of women worked in pregnancy and 10 per cent of these carried on working into the last ten weeks of pregnancy. Another study, carried out in 1979, showed that the proportion of women working in pregnancy had risen to 48 per cent and 75 per cent of these were working into those last ten weeks.

Women have, of course, had a financial incentive to work at least until the twenty-ninth week since 1977, when provisions were made for maternity pay. The first of the six-weekly payments can be made after the twenty-ninth week and women must anyway work up to this point if they wish to retain their right to return to the job after the baby is born.

There is no doubt that many women today work well into pregnancy for financial reasons. In many homes a second salary is not merely useful but essential. In my research for this book I asked more than 100 women what were their main reasons for continuing work during pregnancy. Their jobs were varied: teachers, civil servants, bank clerks, secretaries, nurses, shop assistants, social workers, local government officers, assembly workers, receptionists, accounts clerks, and even a farm worker.

Far and away the most popular reason for a women working through pregnancy was that she needed the money. The second most popular reason was that she intended to return to work after having the baby. There may be financial reasons for going back to work as well as for working in pregnancy, of course, but other evidence suggests that many women return because they *enjoy* their work. Certainly, almost twice as many said they carried on working because they enjoyed their job as said that work was just a way of keeping busy. After all, you don't have to have a high-flying career to feel that work is important to you and the way you feel about yourself.

Whatever your reasons for working through pregnancy – for financial security, your own enjoyment, to safeguard your job or career, or simply because you cannot see why pregnancy could ever be a reason to stop work – it is not always easy to get the balance right, or to convince yourself you are doing the best thing for everyone: yourself, your baby, your family, your boss, and your colleagues.

Even when you think you *have* got everything sorted out in your mind, all kind of things can upset the balance. I can remember my ante-natal teacher talking about labour and birth. Her basic message was that nothing ever goes quite the way you think it will and it is best to be prepared for all eventualities, and to go into the experience with a well-informed but open mind.

Working through pregnancy is much the same. But just as you can prepare for labour, so you can prepare for being a pregnant working woman. That is why I have written this book. I hope it will give you all the information you need to sail through those nine months, but, more than that, I hope it will help you enjoy the time you spend working through pregnancy.

1
Is it safe to work?

First, the good news. There is no conclusive evidence that working through pregnancy can harm you or your baby. Now the bad news. There is no conclusive evidence to prove the opposite either. In other words, the experts don't really know.

However, Professor Geoffrey Chamberlain, whose interest in the subject inspired a symposium on Working and Pregnancy in 1983, and who probably knows as much as anyone about it, says: 'I suspect it does no harm at all.'

So why *do* some doctors still routinely advise women to give up work, even when the pregnancy is proceeding normally?

It is probably part of the 'better safe than sorry' syndrome. But for women who want, or need, to work for as long as possible when they are pregnant (indeed, for women who work at all during pregnancy), this kind of well-meaning approach is not very helpful.

In this chapter I will try to summarize some of the evidence that is currently available on the effects of work in pregnancy, to help you make up your own mind, not just about whether to work or not, but also about whether you might need to modify your working day, switch to other duties or consider stopping work at a particular time.

One of the difficulties in weighing up the evidence is that different studies have concentrated on different things. It is sometimes misleading to compare one study with another, since the women involved in each may not have been the same age, had the same number of children, come from the same social class, kept the same number of ante-natal appointments, or been matched up for any of the other factors which can have some bearing on whether you finally give birth to a healthy bouncing baby or not.

It is also difficult to compare one job with another. Not only may the duties involved vary greatly, but so may the hours worked and the time and effort involved in getting to work. The kind of job you do may be significant, but perhaps as much in the sense that it says something about your background and lifestyle, both of which may influence the way you prepare for pregnancy and look after yourself during it.

In this book the term 'working through pregnancy' refers to paid employment, but most women do other unpaid work in the home. And whether or not you get help at home when you are pregnant, particularly if you already have one or more children, may be just as significant as whether you go out to work or not.

Some studies on working in pregnancy

Researchers have tried to measure the effects of working through pregnancy in a number of different ways. One way is to compare the birth weights of babies born to working and non-working mothers. Another is to look at the numbers of babies born prematurely.

The following studies are some of the examples of the work that has been done on the subject.

Three British studies were carried out in the late 1940s and the early 1950s. Two found evidence of a link between working in the later months of pregnancy and having smaller babies. The third did not.

Recently published information, based on data gathered during the 1958 British Perinatal Mortality Survey, showed that women who worked were no more likely to develop toxaemia than women who did not. Toxaemia is now usually called pre-eclampsia, and is a condition in pregnancy when your blood pressure rises, you retain a lot of fluid and there is protein in your urine. At this stage the danger is to your baby because if the condition is untreated you may go into premature labour.

The figures also show that although mothers who worked were slightly more likely to have babies with a low birth weight than those who did not work, the differences were not statistically significant and other factors seemed more significant than employment: for example, whether it was a first baby, whether the mother was short, whether she smoked, whether she was working-class, and so on.

No evidence was found to suggest there was any difference in the long-term development of children whose mothers worked during pregnancy compared with those whose mothers did not, or who stopped work at different times during pregnancy.

In 1972 the first French national birth survey showed a positive association between employment in pregnancy and low birth weights. In 1976, a second national survey showed no significant association between the two.

Comparing situations

So far, it seems, research has not proved that going to work during pregnancy is in itself harmful. But the kind of job you do, how hard you have to work at it and the conditions in which you work may matter a great deal.

Even the way in which you travel to work may be significant. My own gynaecologist and obstetrician, who did his best to persuade me to take things easy in the latter stages of my first pregnancy, says, 'The women I worry about are the ones who strap-hang in on the tube to the West End, then strap-hang home again, only to turn round and start preparing a meal for their husbands. They are doing two jobs when they should be doing one – and they have an exhausting journey on top of it all.' Or, as Geoffrey Chamberlain puts it, 'Fatigue is probably more significant than work.'

Physically demanding jobs

Doctors have traditionally advised resting during the later stages of pregnancy and if yours is a particularly exhausting job, you might do well to heed this advice.

Dr Frank Hytton of the Medical Research Council's Division of Perinatal Medicine points out that physical activity – particularly if you are standing and in a hot environment – reduces the flow of blood to the womb. Normally this does not matter very much because there is a large margin of safety. But, warns Dr Hytton, 'with severe exercise or if the foetus is already compromised, harm seems likely to occur'.

He bases his opinion on two different pieces of evidence. Firstly, some unborn babies show cardiographic signs of distress when the mother exercises. Secondly, in conditions where the mother habitually works hard in a standing position, there is convincing statistical evidence of reduced foetal growth. For example, a study carried out in 1930 found that women working in the textile mills in India had lighter babies than other Indian women even though they had a higher average energy intake of food. Although their work was not physically arduous, they spent all day standing beside a machine. Furthermore, their babies were almost 200 grams lighter than babies born to the wives of mill workers who lived in the same social conditions but did not themselves work. The study also showed that mill workers who had been laid off as a result of a strike had babies which were almost as big as babies born to non-workers.

Another study, published in 1980, looked at a group of relatively poor Ethiopian women. The women who had to work very hard outside the home each day gained less weight during pregnancy and had much smaller babies than those whose work was considered light.

It is doubtful whether any of us has to work as hard as these women did to keep body and soul together, but another way of measuring the effects of work on your baby is to look at the number of working women who go into premature labour. A study carried out in France during 1977 and 1978 did just that. More than 3400 pregnant women in the city of Lyon and the town of Haguenau took part in a survey which examined whether a woman who carried on working in a strenuous job risked having a premature baby.

Fatigue factors
According to the authors of the report, the fact that a woman works cannot, in itself, be said to be a risk. Globally speaking, housewives have a higher rate of premature birth than working women (7.2 per cent compared with 5.8 per cent). But they believe they were able to identify the 'fatigue factors' which can exist in certain jobs and may tip the balance. It is not just physically demanding work that contitutes a risk: boring, repetitive tasks can cause fatigue too. When drawing up their fatigue chart, the authors looked at different aspects of jobs. As a result of this study, they suggest that if your job involved two or more of the following factors, you could run the risk of having your baby prematurely.

1. Working for more than three hours a day on your feet.
2. Working on an industrial conveyor belt or a machine which demands your making a strenuous effort or coping with vibrations.
3. Carrying loads of more than 10 kilograms.
4. Routine work.
5. Varied tasks which need little attention and tend to be boring and repetitive.
6. Working in a combination (two out of three) of a noisy, cold or very wet atmosphere.
7. Working with certain chemicals.

Working with chemicals
The question of chemicals is a particularly tricky one. More and more chemicals are being used in more and more processes. It has long been established that specific jobs may present specific risks for pregnant women if those jobs involve exposure to toxic substances. Women who work in the chemical or cleaning industries come into contact with powerful chemicals which should be avoided in pregnancy. Pesticides and insecticides can

also be dangerous and certain chemicals used in dyeing, hairdressing and dry cleaning can have side effects on the mother and her unborn child.

The list of these dangerous substances is long and still increasing. It includes carbon tetrachloride, aniline, chlorophene, trichloroethylene, perchloroethylene, chloroform, lead, arsenic, mercury, and the polychlorinated biphenyls. Every year it is estimated that between 700 and 3000 new industrial chemicals are introduced, and nobody knows with any certainty what effects they could have on the human reproductive system.

In 1985 the British Medical Journal published an analysis of stillbirths in the Leicestershire area. It showed that women workers in the leather and shoe industry were twice as likely to have a baby stillborn because of severe congenital malformations than workers in other trades. The evidence suggests that the possible hazard is either from the leather itself or from the chemicals used as adhesives.

The following year, pregnant women working on farms or in veterinary practices were warned by the Scottish Home and Health Department not to help with lambing. This time it was not chemicals that were a problem, but the risk of catching chlamydia, a disease which is common in sheep and can cause women to go into labour dangerously prematurely.

Assessing possible risks
Several difficulties have faced researchers looking for a link between problems in pregnancy and a woman's particular job of work. One is that in the past in England and Wales, for example, the mother's occupation has not been recorded on documents such as the register of births. Also, to make any kind of monitoring exercise manageable, different jobs have to be lumped together under one general heading and this does not necessarily give a clear picture of what the jobs entail. One clerical worker may have a very different job from another clerical worker, for example, as may one professional worker and another.

Even when you *do* know more about a particular job, and there *do* seem to be grounds for thinking it may involve some extra risk to pregnant women, there may still be furious debate as to whether this can be proved or not.

It has been suggested that women working in places like hospitals, where they could be exposed to anaesthetic gases, seem to run a greater risk of having something go wrong with their pregnancy than other women, although there is still much controversy about the extent of the problem, if it does indeed exist. The evidence suggests there may be a greater chance of these women miscarrying, but the Royal College of Obstetricians and Gynaecologists have suggested that the real risk factor is anxiety. In other words, they believe that it is worrying about the possibility of gases causing a miscarriage that is potentially harmful. They have stated, 'There is no direct evidence that atmospheric pollution with anaesthetic gases causes any hazard in human beings.'

As Sheila McKechnie, Health and Safety Officer of the Association of Scientific, Technical and Managerial Staffs, says: 'One is tempted to ask what evidence *would* have to be obtained to show such a "direct" effect and would such evidence in practice be obtainable?'

Working with VDUs

Getting such evidence is not easy, as the recent controversy over VDUs (visual display units linked to a computer) demonstrates. It is not so long ago that people thought X-rays were harmless. Now we know that X-rays may effect the unborn child, particularly in the early stages, and that is the main reason why X-rays should be avoided during pregnancy and why pregnant women are advised not to work in jobs where X-rays are used – for industrial or security purposes, for example. Airport X-rays are carried out with high-voltage sets and image intensifiers, so that there is no risk.

Now people are wondering if VDUs could prove a similar hazard. Since the beginning of the 1980s, when VDUs were first introduced on a large scale, there have been several disturbing reports linking constant use with miscarriages and birth defects.

In Canada, four women VDU operators on the *Toronto Star* newspaper all had deformed babies, and at the Attorney General's office the miscarriage rate for VDU workers over the past four years has been 52 per cent – way above the average.

In Tokyo the general council of Trade Unions, or Sohyo, surveyed VDU workers. Among those questioned were 250 women who had given birth or become pregnant. About 27 per cent of the pregnant women reported complications during pregnancy and 20 per cent reported miscarriages or premature deliveries.

The report also showed that abnormalities increased in proportion to the amount of time spent facing the video displays.

In Britain there has been concern over Department of Employment workers in Runcorn, Cheshire. Of the VDU operators who became pregnant, 36 per cent suffered miscarriages or still-births, or had deformed babies. This compares with a 16 per cent abnormality rate among other workers in the UK.

At the moment nobody knows for sure whether VDUs are harmful to pregnant women, or whether the high rates of miscarriages amongst users can be put down to chance. After all, the available figures are based on very small samples. And if VDUs *are* harmful, why should this be?

One theory is that the VDU screens could be emitting a level of radiation that could affect the growing baby. If there is damage, it is most likely to occur within the first eight weeks, before a woman even knows that she is pregnant.

Some authorities have stated that modern VDUs give off such a low level of radiation that the rays could not possibly affect the foetus. Even if we accept this, it could be that the use of VDUs creates the kind of risk that French researchers identified. Remember the fatigue factor of carrying out boring and repetitive tasks? This is one women's description of working with a VDU. 'Sitting at a VDU for hours at a time can be very boring. You are pressing only a few buttons, and the work requires virtually no physical or mental effort. It's a bit like sitting and watching television for several hours – after a time you feel irritable, jumpy, restless and headachey. You experience that peculiar kind of stress that comes from lack of challenge or excitement.'

Sheila McKechnie has been closely monitoring the health implications of working at a VDU. She says: 'At the moment the evidence connecting these machines with birth defects is very inconclusive, but in view of the concern a few offices are starting to negotiate informal agreements for pregnant women to be allotted other tasks. This is happening more as a result of the anxiety than statistical proof that VDUs cause birth defects.

'It could be that the majority of problems arise because VDUs are making jobs in offices more boring than before. They mean you are only ever doing part of a job, rather than a whole task, so you never have the satisfaction of seeing a particular job through. Also, while operating a machine, you are not interacting with others or taking part in general office life.'

Passive smoking

When I carried out my own survey into pregnancy and work, more than one in eight of the women who took part said they were concerned about having to use VDUs. But three in ten were worried about another, indirect hazard of working – smokers.

Passive smoking (the act of breathing in other people's cigarette smoke) is best avoided if possible. There are several substances in tobacco smoke which can affect your baby, including carbon monoxide and nicotine. The longer you spend in a smoky, ill-ventilated room, the more likely you are to absorb these sunstances, which can cut the supply of oxygen and vital nutrients to your baby and slow down its growth (see chapter 3).

Planning a working pregnancy

In raising all these issues – smokers, VDUs, the use of chemicals, the effects of fatigue, and so on – I do not intend to discourage anyone from the idea of working in pregnancy. Far from it. But I would like to encourage you to think about the work you do and the way you intend to balance the demands of work with the demands of pregnancy. Later chapters will give specific advice on how to do this, but right from the start it is probably a good idea to have some kind of pregnancy plan in mind.

Planning for a working pregnancy, like planning for any pregnancy, should ideally begin before you even conceive. If you are going to work, you should make sure you are as fit as possible so that you and the baby get the best start.

Many experts now feel that you and your partner should allow at least three months and possibly six preparing for pregnancy.

This is the time for you both to stop smoking and drinking and to start eating properly. Unless you are very overweight, don't go on a diet but stick instead to nutritious, balanced meals that steer clear of highly processed foods and foods containing additives.

Go for unrefined foods such as wholemeal bread, wholegrains and wholewheat pasta. Vegetables and fruit will give you vitamins and minerals. Eat them raw and/or unpeeled where possible, but make sure that you wash them well. If you have to cook them, steam rather then boil.

Avoid tinned foods if you can. If you do buy tinned fruit, choose fruit in its own juice rather than in heavy syrup. Try to have fish at least once a week and remember that offal, such as liver and kidneys, is just as nutritious as expensive cuts of meat.

If exercise is not part of your life-style, now is the time to introduce it gradually. Walk instead of taking the car or bus. Go swimming or even dancing.

Medical check-ups
It is probably worth visiting your GP at this stage. Even if he or she cannot give you the pre-conception care and advice you need (although many GPs are now very interested in this subject), you should be able to find out what care is available.

Some of the larger hospitals run pre-conceptual care clinics, and some midwives and health visitors give informal counselling at local clinics. The National Childbirth Trust also offers counselling, as do some voluntary organizations, the best known of which is probably Foresight (see page 184 for their address).

Foresight produces a number of booklets and will also put couples in touch with the nearest doctor running a Foresight Clinic so that they can be screened before they try to conceive. Hair may be analysed to detect toxic metals such as lead, or lack of essential minerals.

Other procedures may include tests for immunity to rubella (German measles), blood pressure tests, urine analysis, blood analysis and a smear. Apart from this, patients are asked for details about their general health, their lifestyle, their eating habits, and contraception. They are given advice on nutrition, alternative contraceptive methods (if necessary) and ways in which to test the metal contamination of their drinking water supplies if it seems that the levels of copper, lead, cadmium, mercury or aluminium in their hair is too high.

Consultation fees vary from clinic to clinic and from case to case, so phone around before opting for a particular clinic.

Assessing your working environment

Having sorted yourself out, it is time to turn your attention to your job. If you are worried that any aspect of your working environment may be harmful to an unborn child, check it out with your doctor, pre-conception counsellor, employer or trade union health and safety representative.

Find out what chemicals you may come into contact with, whether you will be able to get help carrying heavy loads, whether you might be able to work more flexible hours (arriving later and leaving later to miss the rush hour crowd, for instance), or switch to different duties. If you do not want to ask your boss all these questions directly, ask other women in your workplace. They may have experienced a working pregnancy and may know just how flexible or otherwise the job can be. If you belong to a trade union there may be agreements covering working in pregnancy – find out.

If there is a health risk to you or your baby, or your pregnancy that will mean you will not be able to carry out your work adequately, then, providing you have been in the job for long enough, you should be offered suitable alternative work (see chapter 2).

Working with smokers

Ask yourself how you feel about other people smoking, and what will you do about it? Most of the women I interviewed found it very difficult to assert themselves over the question of passive smoking.

One local government officer got her office to buy an electric air purifier. One civil servant says that despite protests she kept the window by her desk open, but adds: 'As a possible result I was off work sick with bronchitis for most of January.' A solicitor said she was more rude to smokers than usual: 'As a result they usually avoided smoking in my office.'

Others, like one copy typist, 'nagged, but got no response'. And many simply put up with it. One journalist said: 'When the smoke got too much I would just leave the room. I didn't feel I could ask people to stop.'

Admittedly it is not easy to ask people to stop doing something for the sake of your baby's health, when they will not even stop for the sake of their own. But it may be worth asking them to smoke less, or to smoke only when the window is open.

It may even be worth asking if you can move to work with non-smokers or if certain areas of the workplace could be designated no-smoking areas, just as certain areas of cinemas or restaurants are. Some employers have already done this.

Reducing risks from VDUs

If you work with VDUs this may also concern you. As one computer operator said, 'It did worry me, but since it was my job I felt there was little I could do about it.' And an accounts clerk who was also worried about using the VDU in her office said: 'I didn't do anything about it because when girls had brought the subject up in the past they were laughed at and told they were fussing over nothing.' However, some women reported that their unions had negotiated agreements giving pregnant women the option of refusing to work on VDUs, and they had exercised this option.

Some women simply tried to use VDUs as little as possible. But if you cannot manage this, you could point out to your firm that screens can now be fitted to VDUs to cut down the level of radiation, and ask if this could be done. Make sure your work place is correctly designed so that you are not having to sit badly or strain to see the screen. Take regular breaks, trying to get away from your screen at least once an hour for ten minutes. Mix in other tasks with VDU work. If you feel that stress, not radiation, is the danger, make sure you take regular breaks.

When to stop work

The next question to ask yourself is: When should I stop? Many women set their sights on the twenty-ninth week of pregnancy as this is the time when they qualify for various rights and benefits. But there are other factors to take into consideration. In some jobs, such as the police force, of course, you are given no choice – a police officer has to stop work after three months. The regulations state: 'In their own interests pregnant officers will not be permitted to perform any duty, including administrative duty, after three months pregnancy and maternity leave will therefore commence six months before the estimated date of confinement.' In other jobs, there may be nothing to stop you working right up until the last minute, although in some cases, such as nursing, you may have to produce a doctor's letter to say you are fit to continue.

Of the women who took part in my survey, 64 per cent worked for more than twenty-nine weeks, although only 10 per cent were still working in the thirty-eighth week or beyond. Less than a quarter (21 per cent) stopped at twenty-nine weeks, when they qualified for maternity pay, and 15 per cent stopped earlier than this, although none stopped before twenty-six weeks.

Women who worked for themselves – a self-employed dental technician and a caterer, for instance – found it hard to hand over responsibility to someone else. Others, like a computer operator and a clerk in an American bank, stayed on to train someone to take over while they were on maternity leave. Teachers found it worthwhile to carry on until the end of a term. A personal secretary stayed at work for as long as possible out of loyalty to her boss who was about to retire. One woman in publishing worked until her mortgage came through – she and her husband needed to show they were earning two incomes to get it!

With hindsight, some women felt they had stayed at work too long. A music teacher who worked for thirty-five weeks said: 'I enjoyed working but I think in a second pregnancy I would not continue to work so close to the birth. I felt extremely tired and clumsy. By the time I'd finished work, all the things I'd put off doing until then just never got done as I was too big and too tired.'

And a clerical officer in the Department of Health and Social Security said: 'I enjoyed working (to the thirty-fourth week) but afterwards I felt I should perhaps have finished earlier. Towards the end of my pregnancy, although I could keep up with the work, I found it very hard getting up in the morning and I was extremely tired in the evenings and went to bed very early'.

'Pregnancy did not affect my work, but working in the latter stages of pregnancy did, I think, affect my general health. In future pregnancies I would finish work at an earlier stage to get the rest I needed.'

On the other hand, some women had no regrets at all. A teacher who worked until the thirty-fourth week said: 'I was extremely bored as soon as I had given up work and was at home all day unable to do very much but wait. A civil servant who also worked until the thirty-fourth week agreed: 'The last few weeks before the baby was born dragged, as I was at home. While I was fully occupied, the weeks went quickly.'

The manageress of a public house who only stopped work a week before her second baby was born said: 'I enjoyed work, mainly because nine months is a long time to wait if you are sat around. I also felt physically and mentally fitter than in my first pregnancy when I gave up work as soon as I could.'

Making the decision
Only *you* can know all the factors involved in deciding when to stop work in pregnancy. Only you can really know how the demands of your job may drain you in mind and body. You will know what the financial pressures are – whether working will be a greater strain than worrying about making ends meet. You will know the kind of help you might expect at home, and the kind of leeway you might get at work.

At the same time, while accepting that pregnancy is not an illness, you should be aware that things may not always go as planned. In the early stages of pregnancy, for instance, you may be unfortunate enough to have a threatened miscarriage. Doctors' attitudes towards a threatened miscarriage vary. Some take the 'if it's going to happen, it will happen whatever you do' view, but you may well be advised to rest. Whether this means taking a few days off work or giving up altogether (particularly if the bleeding happens several times) depends on the situation.

If it turns out that you are expecting twins, you will also be advised to get more rest, and it is unlikely that your pregnancy will last a full forty weeks; on average, twins are born at thirty-seven weeks and triplets at thirty-four weeks.

Nor is it just twins and other multiples who often make an early entrance. In the United Kingdom about 7 per cent of babies are born prematurely.

Another thing which could bring your employment to an abrupt end in the latter stages of pregnancy could be the development of pre-eclampsia, which has already been described. This condition can be dangerous to both mother and baby but these days it is usually spotted in the early stages. However, the most important part of the treatment is rest, and by that I mean proper rest, in bed. If that does not work, then you will be taken into hospital where you may be given other treatments and an intensive watch can be kept on your baby.

Perhaps, in the end, the best advice I can give any woman who is planning to work through pregnancy is this. Use your mind, think about what your work involves, and what your priorities are. Make your plans, but in the end listen to what your body tells you from week to week.

As Geoffrey Chamberlain puts it:

'If you enjoy your job and you are prepared to take sensible steps to make sure that you do not overstretch yourself, then there is no reason for you to give it up.

Many women are so much more conscious of their body and its needs that they know when it is time to stop or reduce the levels of work.'

2
Your rights

In a perfect world, women would be able to choose a job or a career that suited them in every way. One of the things it would offer would be the chance for women who wanted to have children to take generous maternity leave – with pay, of course – before coming back to pick up the threads whenever they felt the time was right. But it isn't a perfect world, of course, and anyway, what might seen perfect for women would probably be a nightmare for employers.

However, the statutory rights that pregnant working women have in Britain are far from satisfactory and in many respects lag way behind the rights enjoyed by many of their European counterparts. On the other hand, some British women, particularly those working in the public sector, may get a far better deal than that laid down by law. The trouble is that few women worry overmuch about maternity rights until they are, or are about to become, pregnant.

I imagine it is a rare women who takes a look at all the maternity packages that have been negotiated with various organizations over the years, works out which bests suits her and gets a job there far enough in advance to qualify for the deal before producing her first child. For those of you reading this chapter it is probably too late to do anything to improve your situation except to make sure that you get everything, however little, to which you are entitled.

Even that is not as easy as it might sound. The Department of Employment produces a booklet on the subject, called *Employment Rights for the Expectant Mother*, but it is hardly light reading. Occasionally, employers will take the trouble to explain your maternity rights once they have formally been told of your pregnancy. Others may not fully understand the law or may leave it to you to find out what the correct procedures are.

A customer accounts clerk, whose baby was born prematurely in the twenty-seventh week of pregnancy, said: 'My employers knew very little about benefits and entitlements. I had to find out all the background and check my wages meticulously to make sure everything was in order.

'I was trying to cope with the possibility of my baby not surviving and the after-effects of a Caesarian, but I got no compassion from my employers. I had to do all the ground work myself. Although my circumstances were unusual, when put to the test my employers knew very little about maternity pay procedures. I was just lucky I had the common-sense to check it all out thoroughly.'

Statutory rights
So what *are* your rights? Women working in pregnancy have four specific rights in law and you may be entitled to all or some of them.

1. Paid time off for ante-natal care
All women, no matter how long they have been working for a particular firm or how big the firm is, have the legal right 'not to be unreasonably refused time off work to receive ante-natal care' and to be paid for this time.

This means that if your ante-natal appointments fall within or near to your working hours, your employer must allow you time off to go to the clinic, doctor's surgery or hospital and keep your appointments. If your employer refuses to do this, or refuses to pay you for the time when you are not at work, then you can complain to an industrial tribunal. Your employer cannot insist that you use up your holiday time, or get there and back in your lunch hour, or make up the time lost later.

You cannot just flit off when you feel like it, however. You have to ask for time off in order to keep an ante-natal appointment and, if, after your first visit, your employer wants documentary evidence, you must produce a certificate stating you are pregnant (it can be signed by a doctor, midwife or health visitor) and a card showing that the appointment has been made.

The law does talk about ante-natal *care* and it could be argued that ante-natal preparation classes are part of this care (see chapter 8). It is certainly worth asking for the time off if it really would suit you best to attend such classes during the time you would normally be at work. However, this is a grey area and if you were refused permission to attend classes there would probably be little you could do about it. So far as I – and all the experts I have talked to – know, there has never been a test case on this issue.

If you have to appeal to a tribunal, you must make your complaint within three months of the disputed appointment. You can get the necessary form from any Jobcentre, employment office or unemployment benefit office.

2. **Protection against dismissal on the grounds of pregnancy**
It seems positively Victorian to think of employers sacking women as soon as they learn they are pregnant, but it still happens.

In theory, if a women is sacked for some reason connected with her pregnancy, she can complain to an industrial tribunal which can order her employer to reinstate her in her old job, re-engage her in a similar one, or make a cash award. Under certain circumstances a boss can claim it was a *fair* dismissal – if, for instance, he can show that the pregnancy made her incapable of doing her job properly or that it is against the law for her to carry on in the job during pregnancy. (A typical case might be that of a radiographer who, by law, cannot be exposed to radiation during pregnancy.)

Under these circumstances, however, an employer first has to try to find a woman alternative work to do while she is pregnant, on similar terms and conditions as her present job, and only if this is impossible can she be fairly dismissed. Even if she is dismissed, her rights to maternity pay and her right to return to her original job after the baby is born are not affected.

But – and it is a big but – you will only get all this protection if you have worked:

(a) full-time (sixteen or more hours a week) for the same employer for at least *one* year, if you started your job before 1st June 1985.
(b) full-time for the same employer for more than *two* years, if you started your job on or after 1st June 1985 *or* if you work for a small firm with fewer than twenty employees
(c) part-time (eight to sixteen hours a week) for the same employer for *five* years or more.

Unfortunately, the change made to the qualifying conditions in 1985 has actually put many pregnant women outside the protection of the law, rather than increasing the numbers covered by it. Between 1st June 1976 and 1st June 1985 you needed to have worked full-time for the same employer for only one year (provided the firm had more than twenty people on the pay-roll) to be safe in the knowledge that you should not get the sack because you were pregnant. But now that the qualifying period has been extended to two years, many women will lose that protection. Some estimates suggest that among unskilled and semi-skilled workers, the numbers covered will drop to between 20 and 33 per cent. And these are women who, more than most, need the money they can earn working through pregnancy.

The change could also have a knock-on effect on reinstatement rights (which are more fully explained later on.) You have the right, for example, to go back to your job, or a broadly similar one, after maternity leave if you have been working full-time for the same employer for two years. But the two-year qualifying period extends up to the twenty-ninth week of pregnancy. As far as reinstatement rights go, it does not matter in theory if you have not clocked up your two years at the start of the pregnancy, provided you have done so before the twenty-ninth week of that pregnancy.

The danger now is that if you announce you are pregnant before you have worked for a particular firm for two years, even though you will have done so by the twenty-ninth week of your pregnancy, you could be sacked at once on the grounds of your pregnancy and thus lose any chance of qualifying for the right to get your job back after the baby is born.

3. **Maternity pay**

A women who qualifies for maternity pay is entitled to get this from her employer for the first six weeks of her absence because of pregnancy. Maternity pay is nine-tenths of a week's pay, less the flat-rate maternity allowance, national insurance contributions and income tax. The money does not come to you from social security, but from your employer, although the firm is entitled to a rebate from the Maternity Pay Fund for the amount paid.

To qualify for maternity pay:

(a) you must have stayed at work until the eleventh week before the week in which the doctors expect you to have your baby (although you could be on holiday or sick leave at this time);
(b) you must, by the beginning of this same week, have worked full-time (sixteen hours or more) for the same employer for two years or part-time (eight to sixteen hours) for five years;
(c) you must write to your employer at least twenty-one days before you stop work, saying you will be absent because of pregnancy.

Your employer can ask you to produce a certificate from a doctor or midwife, stating the expected date of confinement.

If you cannot give twenty-one days' notice – if you have your baby prematurely, for instance – you must write to your employer with details as soon as you reasonably can.

You must comply with all these conditions. If you do not give proper notice or if you stop work too early you may lose your maternity pay. *But you do not have to be intending to return to work after the baby is born to qualify for maternity pay, nor can your employer insist that you leave work eleven weeks before your baby is due.* You can work later into your pregnancy if you like, without losing any of your maternity pay.

This is not always made clear to women; in fact, some employers are not always clear on the point themselves. A handful of women who took part in my survey said that their employers told them they *had* to stop work at twenty-nine weeks. A teacher said: 'I think it should be more widely publicized that you can work longer than twenty-nine weeks if required. I wish I had last time – I was fit enough and the extra money would have been useful.'

If money is one of the main reasons you are working through pregnancy it is certainly worth thinking about working beyond the twenty-ninth week if you feel fit enough. It is true that for every week you work past this time, you lose a weeks' maternity *allowance*, but no matter when you stop, you will still get six weeks' maternity pay. So if you stop at week twenty-nine, you will then get six weeks' maternity pay, plus eighteen weeks' maternity allowance. If you stop at week thirty-four, you will get an extra five weeks' full pay, six weeks' maternity pay, plus thirteen weeks' maternity allowance. And if you work right up to week thirty-nine (and some women do), you will get an extra ten weeks' full pay, six weeks' maternity pay plus eight weeks' maternity allowance.

Given that the maternity allowance is such a pittance (currently £27.95 a week), it does not take a mathematical genius to work out that most women will be far better off financially if they work rather than staying at home to claim the allowance.

4. Returning to work

Most women who qualify for maternity pay will also have the right to return to work with their employer after maternity leave, unless they work in a firm with five or fewer employees. But you must fulfill all the conditions laid down above and, to exercise this right, you must tell your employer three times that you intend to do so.

(a) Tell your employer, when you write to give him three weeks' notice of the date you will stop work, that you intend to come back to work after having the baby. You should also include the expected date of confinement.

(b) Seven weeks after you have had the baby you may get a letter from your employer asking you to confirm that you intend coming back to your job. You must write back within fourteen days or you could lose your right to return.

(c) Finally, at least twenty-one days before you intend to start work again, you must write to let your employer know the date on which you propose to return.

Maternity leave can start from eleven weeks before the baby is due and last for up to twenty-nine weeks after the birth, but you can work later if you want to, or return to work earlier, providing that you give the proper notice. You can extend your leave by four weeks if you are ill, but you will have to send in a medical certificate. You can also delay your return if you are prevented from going back by, for example, a strike. But you must go back as soon as practicable and no later than four weeks after the dispute is over.

Your employer can also ask you to postpone your date of return for up to four weeks, provided he can give you specific reasons and a new start-by date.

Unfortunately, there are no guarantees that you will get your old job back. Employers are allowed to offer you suitable alternative work instead if it has not been 'reasonably practicable' to keep your former job open. What is suitable alternative work? Well may you ask. According to the Department of Employment, it is 'work which is both suitable and appropriate for the employee, and of which the terms and conditions and location are not substantially less favourable than those of her employment before her maternity absence,'

Employers do not legally have to include maternity leave when it comes to totting up things like pension rights, rights to sabbaticals or other length-of-service payments or benefits. The weeks you have off may simply not be counted. But when you return to work you *are* entitled to any all-round pay rises or extra holiday allowances that have been introduced in your absence.

However, maternity leave *does* count towards continuity of employment for general statutory rights such as redundancy or unfair dismissal, nor does your leave break your service in terms of the qualifying period for maternity rights. So if you want to have more children, you do not need to work a further two years after maternity leave in order to qualify for maternity pay and reinstatement after the birth of your next baby.

If you have any trouble getting all or any of your rights, you might try to sort the problem out initially with help from your trade union, if you have one, a local advice or law centre or a Citizen's Advice Bureau.

The Maternity Alliance publishes a check-list of maternity rights at work and can be a useful source of information.

If all else fails, you can appeal to an industrial tribunal but you have to complain within three months of the cause of complaint, and if you are thinking of this line of action it is probably best to get advice from a CAB or law centre in any case.

Other benefits and entitlements
Earlier in this chapter I mentioned the *maternity allowance*. This is a social security benefit and the payment of this weekly allowance depends on your National Insurance contributions. Basically, you should have paid full National Insurance contributions for six months in any one tax year and paid or been credited with a certain number of contributions in the relevant tax year. The rules are pretty complicated, so if you have been working it is worth claiming anyway and your social security office will work out how much of the allowance you should get.

The allowance is generally paid by a book of orders you can cash at the post office for eighteen weeks, beginning eleven weeks before the baby is due, but you will not receive the allowance for any of this time that you are in paid work. If your baby arrives early, you can still receive the allowance for the full eighteen weeks and it will be paid for longer if the baby is late, since it is paid until six weeks after the week in which the baby is actually born.

Claim as soon as possible after the twenty-sixth week of your pregnancy, even if you are still working. If you wait until after you have stopped, you may lose some benefit. You claim the allowance on the same form (BM4) on which you claim the maternity grant. You can get this from your GP, your ante-natal clinic, your health visitor, your social security office, or the CAB. You will also need a certificate of expected confinement (Mat B1), saying when the baby is due. If you have not got this by the time you should claim, don't delay. You can send that on later.

All women, including working women, are entitled to a lump sum *maternity grant* (all £25 of it) providing they have been living in Britain for at least six of the twelve months before the birth of the baby. (There are special regulations for members of the Forces and people working abroad.)

If you are going to claim the maternity allowance you will, no doubt, claim the maternity grant at the same time, but you can actually claim the grant at any time from the twenty-sixth week of pregnancy until three months after the baby is born. If you do wait until after the baby is born you will have to send a copy of the birth certificate rather than a certificate of expected confinement.

Other perks of pregnancy? Well, you do qualify for *free prescriptions and free dental treatment.* Your doctor or midwife will give you a claim form which you send on to your local Family Practitioner Committee. The FPC will send you an exemption certificate which allows you free prescriptions until a year after the date your baby is due. Your dentist will simply give you a form to sign before you start treatment.

There are other benefits and payments available to single mothers and to working women on low pay. At the end of this chapter I have included a list of publications which deal with these entitlements in detail.

All these details relating to maternity rights and provisions were correct at the time of going to press. But the government was proposing to make a number of changes that, if implemented, would have a great impact on the working lives of many pregnant women.

As I explained earlier, a woman's rights to be protected from unfair dismissal, to maternity pay and to reinstatement depend on her having worked a certain number of hours per week for the same firm for a certain number of years.

At the time of writing a woman was deemed to work full-time if she worked sixteen hours or more in the same job a week, and part-time if she worked between eight and sixteen hours. But, under the new proposals, the number of hours per week you would need to work to qualify would go up to twenty and twelve respectively.

In addition, when it comes to reinstatement, whereas at present only firms that have five employees or fewer are under no obligation to allow a woman to return to work after having a baby, under the new proposals, firms employing *ten* people or fewer will no longer be obliged to do so.

Bearing in mind the patterns of female employment, the EOC has predicted it is likely that if these proposals become law the majority of women will not qualify for the basic right of reinstatement.

The government was also proposing to make changes in the way the statutory maternity allowance is operated, by transferring the responsibility of payment from the DHSS to employers, although the DHSS would continue to operate a maternity allowance scheme for the self-employed, the out-of-work and women not eligible to be paid by their employers.

The one good thing about the proposals is that the period of payment would be more flexible than at present. A woman could work until the sixth week before the expected birth of her baby and still get the full eighteen weeks' allowance, whereas, at present, she loses one week's allowance for any week she works after the twenty-ninth of her pregnancy.

But the EOC point out that there would be other disadvantages. For example, it is proposed to make the allowance taxable (it is not at the moment) and the criteria for eligibility means that a significant number of women would not qualify, nor would some of these qualify for the residual benefits.

Other problems may arise out of confusion as employers would have to work out all the various factors involved in awarding both the maternity allowance and maternity pay. As a result some women might lose money they were entitled to. This is not a wild guess – this kind of thing happens already.

A survey of women's experience of maternity rights, funded by the Department of Employment and published in 1980, found that a significant proportion of women employed by very small firms who qualified for maternity pay, failed to receive the money to which they were entitled.

How we compare with Europe

Whichever way you look at it, working women in Britain do not get a particularly good deal when they are pregnant, unless they are fortunate enough to work for a company which offers a package exceeding the statutory requirements. At first glance, it might appear that the total of forty weeks which a woman is allowed to take off work (providing she qualifies for the right) is generous. But of this time, only six weeks is covered by maternity pay. Women in other countries may have less statutory leave, but longer *paid* leave. In West Germany, for instance, women are entitled to have six weeks off before the baby is due and a further eight weeks after it is born; during these fourteen weeks they get maternity pay equivalent to their full salary.

In Britain, women can get up to eighteen weeks' maternity allowance at a flat rate. In Italy, where a woman gets a basic five months' leave plus an option of a further six months' leave at any time up to the child's first birthday, the maternity allowance is 80 per cent of her earnings for the five months, and 30 per cent of her earnings for the further six.

Unlike Britain, some countries also give workers rights to paternity or parental leave. In Belgium, for instance, three months' unpaid leave can be taken by either parent in the year following the birth. Mothers are entitled to social security during this period. In France, if a parent has worked for at least a year for a firm employing more than 100 people, he or she can take up to two years' unpaid leave to look after a child under the age of three. Women have to tack this on to the end of their maternity leave. Fathers can begin parental leave two months after the birth of their child.

Problems with the system in Britain

A number of women who took part in my survey complained about the inflexibility of the system that exists in this country. Some said they would have liked to have taken some leave in the early stages of pregnancy, when they were feeling at their most sick and tired, and to have made up those weeks later on. As one said: 'You don't usually need eleven weeks off in one big lump before the baby is born, but being able to take a few of those weeks in the first few months of pregnancy could be a big help.'

Even more women complained bitterly that they did not qualify for maternity pay, maternity allowance or the right to get their job back. A care assistant said: 'I felt bitter about not being able to claim benefits. I missed out by about four contributions although I've worked on and off since I was fifteen years old.' Others felt they were forced to work later into their pregnancies either because they needed all the cash they could get while they were still working, or because they hoped this would persuade their employers to hold their job open for them.

A local government officer worked until thirty-six weeks 'because I didn't qualify for maternity pay' and a journalist worked up until the time she had her first labour pains in the office. She said: 'I'd only had the job three months so I had no maternity rights and I had to prove I would carry on regardless.'

A solicitor worked for thirty-seven weeks (using up her holiday allowance to enable her to put in shorter hours in the last five weeks) because she did not qualify for pay or reinstatement rights. She says: 'In fact, I missed the magic day by about five weeks. I feel that this was very unfair, particularly over the pay, as I had been working and paying National Insurance contributions for about ten years. I had only changed my job because my husband had to change his, and we had to move.'

The Equal Opportunities Commission has been saying for ages that the conditions laid down concerning a woman's right to pay, leave and reinstatement are far tougher than those found in other countries. In one comparison of parental leave provisions in fourteen countries, Britain came out worst. Elsewhere it was the norm for a woman to qualify if she had been working for about a year, not necessarily with the same employer.

There are a number of reasons why women find it hard to clock up the length of service required to qualify for the rights to keep their job during pregnancy, to get maternity pay and be able to return to work after having the baby.

Women who stay on at school and then go on to do further training or to get higher qualifications, may find themselves starting their first job in their early twenties. Women who want a career may find that promotion does not come in easy stages – it may involve switching from firm to firm. So the career girl who wants a baby before she is thirty may find it difficult to complete two years with one employer.

In any case, jobs are often hard to find these days. Redundancies are common. A woman who has lost her job may take something else temporarily, only to leave when something better comes up. Often it is the husband's job which determines where the family has to live and where the woman can work. Chopping and changing, for whatever reason, means a woman forfeits any time spent working for a previous employer.

Women with older children may have to take part-time jobs (and therefore have to work five years for the same employer). They may have to stop work in the holidays, or if a child is sick.

Will things change?

Changes in the law to make things better for the pregnant working woman seem unlikely – in fact, as discussed earlier, they may make things worse. A draft directive giving parental leave has reached an advanced stage of the EEC's law-making process, but it does not seem likely to move any further in the foreseeable future. Certainly, at the time of writing, the Conservative government has no intention of letting the draft directive, which would give working parents at least three months' full or six months' part-time leave following maternity leave to take care of a child under two, become EEC law.

Peter Bottomley, the Under-Secretary of State at the Department of Employment in June 1985, said: 'The Government's view is that the matters covered by the draft directive are best dealt with between employers and employees according to their own priorities, needs and circumstances rather than by Government or Community intervention.

'The Government are also concerned at the potential costs and administrative burden such a measure would impose on employers and we strongly believe that here and in Europe we should be focussing our energies and efforts on the main problem that faces us all – unemployment – rather than on improving the position of people who already have jobs.'

It is all very well for ministers to state blithely that improvements to the statutory maternity provisions are a matter for individual employers and their employees. The fact is that most organizations stick to the legal minimum and there is little evidence that progress is being made voluntarily. A report on maternity and paternity leave produced in 1985 by Incomes Data Services, for example, found that 'developments over the past four years have been slight and scarce'.

Who fares best?

However, the report did point out that women working in the public sector generally had better deals than those working in the private sector. This fact, one suspects, is not unconnecected to the levels of trade union activity in both, although it is also true to say that many public employers are reluctant to lose qualified staff such as teachers and nurses simply because they have had babies.

The IDS report gave some examples of improved maternity packages. In the Civil Service, for example, women qualify for three months' paid maternity leave if they
(a) state that they intend to return to work in the Civil Service;
(b) agree to pay back their maternity pay if they do not return to complete a month's service;
(c) are working at the time maternity leave begins and have been working for at least one year during the three years before;
(d) work fifteen hours or more a week;
(e) are not employed on a casual basis or a fixed-term contract of less than two years.

The maximum amount of maternity leave is fifty-two weeks. However, women have the alternative of taking a 'baby break' since ex-civil servants are given priority in job vacancies if they wish to return within three years of leaving.

Thousands of women are employed full and part-time by local authorities, so it is not surprising that provisions for maternity pay and leave are fairly generous compared with the statutory schemes.

Even so, some local authorities have better packages than others. In the London borough of Islington, for instance, you do not have to work any particular length of time to qualify; you get six weeks' paid leave at 90 per cent of your weekly wage, then twenty-four weeks on half pay; and you have the right to return full or part-time up to five years from the date the baby was born.

Pressures for improvement

Although the Conservative government has made it plain that they are less than keen to extend the rights of pregnant working women, the unions continue to press claims for better maternity provisions. The TUC has called for maternity leave and pay to be available for a woman who has worked for an employer for only six months; for maternity pay to be paid for eighteen weeks; and for the maternity allowance period to be available with greater flexibility between the period before and after confinement.

Individual unions, such as the Transport and General Workers' Union, have suggested that their negotiators ask for other things as well, like the right to return to part-time work, an extension of maternity leave, and less complicated procedures of notifying employers that you will be taking maternity leave and intend to return to work.

Certainly thousands of working women would benefit if some or all of these changes to the law were to take place, but in the current climate it seems unlikely to happen. However, there is one encouraging development that may, at least, protect some women from being sacked in pregnancy.

The Equal Opportunities Commission gets a regular number of complaints from women who have been dismissed when they announce they are pregnant. The Employment Protection Act now offers no help to such women unless they have been working for the same firm for two years, but the EOC has been working hard to ensure that they should, at least, be protected by the Sex Discrimination Act, if they are sacked for reasons solely relating to pregnancy and cannot meet the hours and service requirements.

A case brought in 1979 had long proved a stumbling block to progress in this area, because the industrial tribunal which ruled in the case decided that dismissal because of pregnancy was *not* unlawful within the meaning of the Sex Discrimination Act.

Then came the cases of Sandra Heyes, a part-time barmaid from Cleveland, and Caroline Maughan, a London trainee court clerk. Both were dismissed shortly after starting jobs because they were pregnant. They could not claim under the Employment Protection Act because neither had worked for the qualifying period. However, with the EOC's support, they brought separate claims under the Sex Discrimination Act.

At first both lost their cases because of the previous ruling, but an Employment Appeal Tribunal, to whom they appealed, decided there should be new hearings, and this has opened the way for women to take action in such cases under the Sex Discrimination Act.

Even though this is a step in the right direction, the situation for many women working in pregnancy is far from ideal. But until we get a better, simpler, fairer deal, the best we can all do is make sure make sure we know about the rights we do have, make sure we claim all we are entitled to and support those who are campaigning and negotiating for improvements. Some useful leaflets and contacts are listed on page 184.

3
Early days

When is the ideal time to break the news at work that you are expecting a baby? As soon as your pregnancy test shows positive? Or only when people start to comment on the fact that you seem to be putting on a lot of weight?

There probably isn't an ideal time. Only you can judge what seems best in your own circumstances, but there are a number of factors worth bearing in mind.

The possibility of a miscarriage
I was actually offered a job about a week after I learned I was pregnant. Under the circumstances, I felt it only fair to let the editor concerned know that I would eventually need some

maternity leave. I was delighted to be told that the pregnancy made no difference to the job offer and so I started work in a new office where everyone knew about the forthcoming baby.

A month later I had a miscarriage, and for some weeks afterwards I had to go through the painful (for me) and embarrassing (for them) task of explaining this to well-meaning colleagues who knew I had been expecting a baby but not that I had lost it. The next time I was pregnant I kept very quiet about it until well past the early weeks.

Miscarriage is not something many people talk to expectant mothers about, understandably enough. Yet it is fairly common, as you soon realize *after* you have gone through the experience. Only then do other women sympathize by telling you that it happened to them.

About one in five of all pregnancies end in a miscarriage and three-quarters of these occur in the first twelve weeks of pregnancy.

No one knows what causes most miscarriages but there is no reason to suppose that because you have a miscarriage once, you will not have a straightforward pregnancy the next time. But although there is no evidence to show that working can cause a miscarriage, if you find yourself suffering from a threatened miscarriage (in other words, you have vaginal bleeding which may or may not be accompanied with pain), you will probably be advised to stop work and stay in bed until the bleeding stops.

Even then not all women feel it necessary to tell their employers exactly what is going on. A solicitor told me that she had an early threatened miscarriage which involved about a week off work before the pregnancy had been 'announced'. She says: 'I told the company that I had had a stomach upset and I think I persuaded my doctor to write "abdominal pains" on my certificate, which was true although not the whole truth.

'The main problem was that the company had recently been taken over by another firm and I didn't want them to get the impression that I might be leaving at any time. After all, it was possible that I might never have a baby and might be working there for another ten years. I didn't want them to have any attitudes towards me that might have affected my partnership prospects. In fact, I didn't tell anyone, including my mother, that I was pregnant until I was well past the four months stage.'

The reaction of colleagues
The possibility of miscarriage is not the only reason why some women wait a while before spreading the good news. Doubts about the way their bosses and/or colleagues might treat them are sometimes involved. As I explained in the previous chapter, it is not unknown for a woman to be sacked when she is pregnant and she may have no legal redress.

A magazine journalist, who had only been at her job for three months before becoming pregnant, and so had few maternity rights, felt she had to prove her worth to keep her job open. She says: 'I purposely didn't tell anyone I was pregnant till six months in case I was just treated as a seething mass of hormones.'

On the other hand, the early months of pregnancy may not be easy for the working woman. Outwardly you may look much the same as usual, but your body is undergoing all kinds of changes and you may feel far from your normal self. You might feel it would be helpful if those around you knew what was happening, too.

Coping with tiredness
One of the most common symptons of early pregnancy is tiredness. Unless you have experienced it it is hard to describe. Even if your working day has been relatively easy, you find yourself absolutely exhausted in the evenings – I used to fall asleep on the sofa at eight-thirty every night without fail. But the feeling of lethargy can persist through the day, too. In fact, two out of three women who took part in my survey on pregnancy and work reported that they found work more difficult than usual because they were very tired.

Doctors suggest that this lack of energy in the early stages of pregnancy is frequently associated with a fall in blood pressure as a result of hormonal changes, and suggest that this may be one of Mother Nature's little ways of ensuring that you rest during this vital stage.

The best advice is not to fight fatigue but to give in to it. Get your priorities right. So you go to bed before the Nine O'Clock News – so what? So you become a social recluse for a few weeks –

you can start going out and about again in the middle months when the tiredness usually lifts.

Sickness during pregnancy

Colleagues at work might not notice your lethargy, particularly if it strikes in the early evening, and even if they do, they might easily put it down to late nights or a hectic social life. However, another of the common symptoms of early pregnancy can often be virtually impossible to keep to yourself: so-called morning sickness.

I say 'so-called' because morning sickness may occur just as readily in the evening or any time of the day and you may not actually be sick, simply nauseous. It is estimated that up to 70 per cent of pregnant women suffer from some form of this complaint, their symptoms ranging from mild nausea in the morning to all-day nausea and frequent vomiting. In fact, less than 10 per cent of women are sick only in the morning.

No one knows for sure why some women feel sick, or are sick, in pregnancy. In the past, many doctors put it down to psychological reasons, although few women who have suffered from it are easily convinced it is 'all in the mind'. Now it is thought that stress may make it worse, but it is actually due to a disturbance in the normal working of the body.

One theory suggests that pregnancy sickness may be related to the levels of the hormone HCG in your body, which are usually at the highest when pregnancy sickness is at its worst. This hormone is produced by the growing embryo in large amounts, and one of its functions is to ensure that the developing baby stays in the womb for the first few weeks of pregnancy. Professor Geoffrey Chamberlain says: 'Once foetal growth is established by about ten to twelve weeks, the concentrations of the hormone are reduced and the sickness commonly gets better.'

Some doctors are less sympathetic than they might be over the question of morning sickness, partly because there is a feeling in the medical profession that the sicker you feel, the more stable your pregnancy. But it has to be said that many women, myself included, have gone through a pregnancy without feeling the slightest queasy sensation and had no problems with morning sickness whatsoever.

Sickness and travel

On the other hand, sickness can create real difficulties if you are working, even if it does no harm in the long run to the baby itself.

A number of the women who took part in my survey complained about sickness. One nurse said she suffered from nausea and vomiting for the first four months and her bus journey to work seemed to make this much worse. A private secretary had all-day sickness in the early months. 'I wasn't often actually sick, but I felt dreadful all the time.' (Her journey to work involved a mile walk, a train journey, a tube journey then a ten-minute walk the other end.)

A secondary school teacher said she had to leave many a class suddenly to be sick. And a trainee clinical psychologist suffered so badly from vomiting, which persisted occasionally right up to the end of the pregnancy, that she had to stop work and continue her studies at home. She said: 'The last placement I was on necessitated travel three days a week by train, bus or coach. I finally gave up when I was sick on the coach.'

Coping at work

Colleagues at work are not always as sympathetic as they might be. A civil servant working for the DHSS said: 'I am glad overall that I did work through pregnancy as it did keep my mind occupied. I just wish "the office" had realized that I was pregnant, and not just being a nuisance deliberately.

'I suffered with morning sickness, but because this was seen as "normal" in pregnancy, they seemed surprised that I needed to spend any time away from my desk. I assumed they wanted me to vomit into my waste paper bin!'

Another woman, a virologist, found it even harder coping with sickness in the early stages of her pregnancy as she was reluctant to tell her boss or colleagues that she was expecting a baby.

She said: 'As I was thirty-seven I had decided to have some tests done to make sure the baby was normal. If there were any problems I had decided I would have an abortion. The tests themselves carry a slight miscarriage risk, and at my age I felt there was a possibility I might miscarry anyway. So I really did not want to say anything to anyone until I knew that the pregnancy was going to go ahead.

'But it really was awful trying to hide my condition. The sickness was so bad that I couldn't keep any food down for long. A typical day would start with my husband bringing me toast and weak tea in bed. I'd nibble and sip slowly but as soon as I got up I'd bring the whole lot back. Then I'd have a bowl of cereal. Maybe I'd hang on to that until midday. I'd try some vegetable soup at lunchtime – then I'd be sick again. I munched cream crackers through the afternoon which helped a bit, but I'd be sick again at four or five o'clock.

'I don't think I was ever sick less than four times a day in the first twelve weeks, and I felt sick all the time. My only pleasure was in going to bed because then I didn't feel sick.

'Getting to the loo was the worst problem. A couple of times I had to use the sink in the lab and pray no one would come in. And I used to go to the loo farthest away, which fewer people used, if I could get there in time. If someone came in while I was being sick I had to flush the loo so they wouldn't hear.

'I suppose it did affect my work a bit. But after I'd been sick I'd feel fine for half an hour and I'd work like mad to get twice as much work done then. And when I was really busy it did take my mind off feeling sick, whereas at weekends that was all I thought about. On balance, I'm glad I was working, despite the difficulties.'

Diet and rest

If hormone levels play a part in pregnancy sickness, so too may your diet (both before pregnancy and during the early weeks) and your way of life. If you are not getting enough rest and are under a lot of stress, the sickness may be worse than it would otherwise have been. If you have a long or tiring journey to and from work, the problem may be exacerbated.

One of the problems that cropped up over and over again in my survey was the reluctance of the general public to offer seats on buses or trains to women, even when they were obviously pregnant. The situation is worse when you don't even have a bump to indicated your condition. Yet this may be the very time when you are feeling your grottiest and need to be able to sit down.

I found that people never refused a direct request. In fact, if I spoke directly to someone along the lines of: 'I wonder if I could sit down – you see, I'm pregnant and I'm feeling sick', that always did the trick. Not only did I get a seat but the crowds positively edged away! And I never felt a bit guilty about the fact that I wasn't feeling at all nauseous!

Being assertive is one way you can help yourself, but there are other things worth trying. Some women find it helpful to wear clothes which are not tight round the waist. Fresh air and a little gentle exercise, like a short walk at lunchtime, could help too.

Some doctors recommend a supplement of vitamin B6, so it might be worth eating foods which are high in the vitamin, such as wholegrain cereals, wheatgerm, bananas or yeast extract.

You may find that eating little but often, instead of sticking to a regular three meals a day, makes you feel a bit better. It is a good idea to eat more unrefined carbohydrates such as wholemeal bread and pasta, fresh fruit, potatoes, and to cut down on foods which are high in fat or protein. Avoid fried and fatty meals and choose chicken or fish instead of red meat.

Nibble some dry toast or a plain biscuit *before* you sit up and get out of bed in the mornings. Have a snack before you go to bed, even if you do not feel like it. It may make you feel less sick in the morning.

Medical help
Sucking a boiled sweet may help to stop you feeling sick – or, anyway, *being* sick – when you are travelling. If the sickness is really bad you should discuss it with your doctor, who may prescribe a suitable drug. Some women consult homoeopathic doctors or pharmacists who will prescibe an individual homoeopathic remedy. You can find out where your nearest homoeopathic doctor or pharmacist is by contacting the British Homoeopathic Association. (See page 184 for their address).

The most commonly prescribed homeopathic remedy for sickness and nausea during pregnancy is ipecacuana, but there are other remedies which may be more appropriate in individual cases. Only by listening to a complete list of syptoms will the doctor know what it is best to prescibe. There are some NHS homoeopathic GPs, but you have to live in their catchment area before you can transfer to their NHS list. You can see any homoeopathic doctor privately, of course. There is no set scale of charges so you should check with the receptionist when making an appointment. The cost of a course of tablets itself is not expensive (probably less than an NHS prescription, although you are, of course, exempt from NHS charges during pregnancy).

Irritation of the bladder
If you suffer badly from sickness in pregnancy, you probably feel too wretched to be particularly embarrassed by it. There are other things which can cause embarrassment, however, the most common of which, in the early days, is having to keep going to the loo.

Doctors used to say this was because the growing baby and enlarging uterus pressed on the bladder in the early weeks while the uterus was still contained within the pelvis. Now, however, they say that it is the hormones produced in pregnancy which influence the muscular wall of the bladder and cause a mild irritation long before the growing uterus is big enough to press on the bladder itself. In addition to this, you actually pass more urine during pregnancy: as the blood flow through each kidney is increased by up to 50 per cent, so more water is filtered out of the blood.

You will not solve the problem by drinking less. In fact, it is important to keep your fluid intake up, as during pregnancy there is a greater risk of a urinary tract infection. So there is little you can do except to plan your day so that you are never far from a handy loo, and if your job involves a great deal of travelling make allowances for extra stops en route if necessary.

Fainting
Another hazard in the early days is fainting. I once arranged an interview over lunch in a London restaurant in the early stages of my first pregnancy only to have to be escorted out into the fresh air before I fell face down into the first course. In fact, pregnant women are more likely to feel faint if they have to stand for any length of time – queuing for a bus, for instance.

If you do start to feel faint it can help to take a few deep breaths but if this does not work, the best thing is either to lie down or to sit and let your head drop down between your knees. Admittedly neither is very elegant, but then nor is collapsing in a heap. To prevent fainting you should keep your blood circulating. If you have to stand for a long time, move your weight from one foot to the other.

Arranging flexible hours
For women who are working, early pregnancy can be the most difficult time. Far from feeling, or looking, like the radiant mums-to-be you see pictured in catalogues or advertisements for maternity clothes or baby goods you may be physically rather wretched, however pleased you are to be pregnant. And if you have been planning to work through your pregnancy you may even be feeling pretty discouraged about the whole prospect. But you should take heart. For most women the middle months are a different story altogether.

As a research nurse who worked for thirty-two weeks in her pregnancy put it: 'I found the first four months very difficult because of tiredness and nausea. But I felt so much better later that I probably could have continued to work longer.

'If I had not had a flexible kind of job with considerate bosses I seriously wonder if I would have continued working beyond the third month – although from the fifth month onwards I was so full of energy I caught up with all the work that had been allowed to fall behind.

'I sometimes wonder if there is not a case for more maternity leave early in pregnancy and less later on, even if the time were taken in half days or a shorter working week.'

There seems little likelihood of this kind of flexibility being introduced into the already complex provisions for maternity leave and pay. If you are due any holiday time, though, it might be worth finding out if you can take this early on in your pregnancy.

If your journey to and from work is making life more difficult for you it may also be worth finding out if you can alter your working hours slightly, so you can avoid having to travel to or from work during the rush hours.

Some women who worked in companies operating Flexitime say that they were able to work the system to their advantage. A civil servant said: 'I think I managed only because we had flexible hours. On a bad day I could go in late and come home early and then on a good day I could put in extra hours.'

Resting at work

For many women, this kind of arrangement is not possible because they work set shifts in a factory or hospital, serve in a shop which has set opening hours, and so on. Under these circumstances the most you can do is to take advantage of the breaks you get. Don't use your lunch hour to do the shopping if you can avoid it. Find out if there is a quiet room, such as a first-aid room or a conference room, where you can lie down or put your feet up.

From the replies I got to the survey, it seems that employers are not very good at providing facilites like a rest room for their workers, pregnant or not. Fewer than one in four women who responded said they had anywhere they could go and put their feet up, and even those who said they were able to rest often added that there were no official facilities.

There is no need to be defeatist about it, however. Often employers simply do not realize that there is a need for something like a rest room, and you can hardly expect them to be mind readers, so it is best to ask if any arrangements could be made.

I knew there was a duty nurse and a first-aid room on the newspaper where I worked, but it was not until I asked about it that I found there were beds there. So when I felt really tired I would spend a quiet lunch hour with my feet up and my eyes closed, and I felt all the better for it in the afternoon.

Other women who were not so lucky made the most of what there was available. An office worker, who shared her office with another woman, used to lock the door, take the phone off the hook and pretend she was out so she could have a quiet and uninterrupted hour to relax by herself. A factory worker who was pregnant during the summer used to go out and lie down on the nearby sports field. Another office worker used to go out to the car park, put the passenger seat back as far as it would go in her car and have a gentle snooze.

The dangers of smoking

The early weeks are vital ones for your developing baby and you may have to adapt your pre-pregnancy work habits to give it the best start. If you smoke, for instance, and you did not give up while planning for your pregnancy, you should redouble your efforts now. After all, you have the best possible motive. Even if you have never managed to give up cigarettes for your own health, you should try for the health of your baby.

There are three substances involved in cigarette smoking that can put your baby at risk: carbon monoxide, cyanide and nicotine. Obviously, while you are inhaling smoke you are cutting down your oxygen supply and, in turn, the baby's. Carbon monoxide combines with the haemoglobin in the blood and this, too, reduces the amount of oxygen that is available for the baby. Cyanide is a toxic substance, and it also combines with important nutrients, limiting their supply to the baby. On top of this, nicotine passes from your blood stream into the baby's making the foetal heart speed up and interrupting the respiratory movements which are a rehearsal for breathing – it is as if the baby coughs and splutters. At the same time, nicotine interferes with the efficiency of the placenta, making the blood vessels in the placenta and cord constrict, so that less oxygen and fewer vital nutrients reach the baby.

There is evidence to show that mothers who smoke have smaller babies than mothers who do not, and that the baby's weight drops in direct relation to the number of cigarettes smoked. Of course you will always meet women who claim to have smoked like a chimney during pregnancy and still given birth to a whopping ten-pounder, but the statistics clearly show that the babies of smoking women do not get the best possible nutrition in the womb. And it is no good telling yourself that having a smaller baby will mean having an easier labour – there is no such guarantee.

Smoking after the fourth month of pregnancy can cause premature births. Even if babies are born at term, they may be so small for their dates that they have to be cared for in a special-care baby unit. Smoking also increases the chances of bleeding during pregnancy, miscarriage, premature rupture of the membranes, haemorrhage before or early in labour or after delivery, stillbirth and the death of the baby in the week following delivery.

The more you smoke, the more you risk this kind of tragedy.

Giving up smoking

So what is the best way to kick the habit? Fortunately, many women feel so queasy in early pregnancy that they cannot face the thought of a cigarette. Non-smokers find that even the smell of someone else smoking is unbearable. Even smokers who do not suffer from pregnancy sickness may find they stop smoking because cigarettes no longer taste the same. It is as if the body has its own ways of protecting the baby.

However, if you are a smoker and you still have the urge to smoke, there are ways of beating it. Giving up cigarettes may not be as hard as you think. Surveys have shown that over 65 per cent of ex-smokers say that stopping was surprisingly easy.

Smokers smoke a lot of cigarettes from sheer habit. They light up when they pick up the phone, sit down with a cup of coffee, put a sheet of paper in the typewriter. Train yourself to do something else instead. Chew matches. Get a doodle pad, get out some knitting to keep your hands busy during coffee breaks.

It often helps to stop at the same time as someone else, even to have a bet on it. Passive smoking can be harmful too, as I mentioned earlier, so it is a good idea to encourage your partner or your work colleagues to stop smoking.

If you are really finding it difficult to stop, talk to your doctor. He may suggest switching to a chewing gum which contains a small amount of nicotine. This will not have such a bad effect on your baby and may help you over the withdrawal stage of the first few weeks.

Many women say they smoke when they are under pressure, because a cigarette helps them calm down. When they are pregnant they worry that they cannot manage without the cigarettes that help them through these moments of stress but, at the same time, they feel incredibly guilty about smoking.

Feelings of guilt and emotional stress can affect your heart rate, your blood pressure, your breathing, and adrenaline levels in your bloodstream, all of which may affect your baby. So the question is, how much stress should you put up with in order to stop smoking?

If you cannot give up altogether it may be possible to cut right down, even to the extent of lighting up the occasional cigarette and stubbing it out again after a few puffs. But if you can find other ways of coping with stress, so much the better.

Relaxation techniques
Some women have found relaxation techniques useful. One way

of relaxing is to lie down in a quiet, dimly lit room, flat on your back with your legs slightly apart and your hands, palms up, by your sides. (Some women find lying on their back uncomfortable in pregnancy; if that applies to you, find a comfortable alternative position, such as on your side.) Close your eyes. Starting with your toes and your feet, deliberately tense the muscles in each part of your body in turn, and then let them relax. Gradually work all the way up to your scalp, not forgetting the muscles of your pelvic floor and your mouth.

When you are completely relaxed just concentrate on listening to the pattern of your breathing, without disturbing it, and try to let your mind go as limp as your body. Think of the tension draining out of your body, into the floor. Imagine yourself getting heavier and heavier.

Of course, I am not suggesting that you lie down on the office floor whenever you feel like a cigarette, but if you practise this tense-relax technique at home, once a day for fifteen minutes, you should soon be able to relax at any time, anywhere, without having to run through the tension exercises first. You can then try to relax consciously instead of reaching for a cigarette in moments of stress at work.

Cutting down on alcohol

Another work-related hazard, particularly for women whose jobs involve entertaining clients, is alcohol. After smoking, alcohol is probably the second most common environmental cause of problems in an unborn baby's development. If you drink heavily during pregnancy (five to six drinks a day) you run a much greater risk of having a baby suffering from foetal alcohol syndrome, which is a condition where the baby has certain facial deformities and is mentally and physically retarded. But even if you drink much less than this, you could still harm your baby.

There is no safe amount of alcohol that can be drunk in pregnancy. Even the smallest dose gets passed on to the baby. The danger to your child is greatest during the very early weeks and it is probably wise not to drink at all during this time. Studies in the UK have shown that women who had more than ten drinks a week, before as well as during pregnancy, doubled their risk of a low birthweight baby, compared with women who had fewer than five drinks a week. So if you do decide to have the odd drink later on, make sure it really *is* an occasional drink and avoid binges, so that your blood alcohol level stays low all the time.

It is not too difficult these days to steer clear of alcohol if you really want to. The dangers of drinking in pregnancy have been quite widely publicized so most people will accept pregnancy as a reasonable excuse for not wanting to drink. Even if you have not announced your pregnancy, there are other socially acceptable excuses. You could say you are on a diet, or allergic to alcohol or simply that you have a rule not to drink during working hours.

You may find that you do not have to explain yourself at all. If someone asks you what you want to drink, choose mineral water or fruit juice or, if you are in a pub, one of the new alcohol-free beers.

There are still people who think no one can relax and enjoy themselves unless they are under the influence of alcohol, so if you have to deal with this kind of bore – at a Christmas party, for instance – agree to have one glass of wine, then keep it topped up with soda. Or get yourself a tonic with ice and lemon – who is to know there is no gin in it?

Eating the right foods
The best way to protect your baby from the ill-effects of drinking and smoking is to cut out cigarettes and alcohol altogether, but eating the right food can help too. Even if you do not smoke or drink during pregnancy, the kind of food you eat is important.

The trouble is that if you are working, it is not always easy to eat well. A survey carried out in October 1985 into company canteens suggested that eating at work could seriously damage your health. It showed that fatty foods were being dished out every day to millions of workers with no regard for a healthy diet. Four out of five works canteens did not even serve up what the Labour Research Department called 'the absolute basics' for healthy eating: a choice of two hot dishes, cooked potatoes, brown bread and fresh fruit.

The TUC has been encouraging unions to make agreements which include special workplace health arrangements for pregnant women. They suggest that unions should press for orange juice and other foods particularly beneficial for pregnant women to be available in staff canteens. If you belong to a union and this kind of diet is not available, approach your representative to see if anything can be done.

If you do not eat in an office canteen, but shop for snacks at lunchtime, make sure you buy the right things. Go for wholemeal sandwiches, salads, cheese, fresh fruit. Skip the take-away burgers and sausage rolls. But *don't* skip lunch altogether because it seems like too much hassle.

The other problem, particularly in the early days, is that you may feel too tired to do much cooking when you get home in the evening. Even so, you can eat well without too much trouble. Cheese on wholemeal toast and an orange is just as easy as a tin of spaghetti and a tin of peaches, and far better for you.

What you and your baby need is a balanced diet. The easiest way to ensure you get this is to think of food in four main groups: meat and its alternatives; fruit and vegetables; bread and cereals; milk and milk products.

Roughly speaking, you should have two servings a day from group one, five a day from group two, five a day from group three and about a pint of milk, or the equivalent, a day.

A serving from group one might be 4 ounces of meat, or a cup of unsalted nuts, or two eggs. A serving from group two might be a bowl of cereal or a slice of wholemeal bread. A serving from group three might be an orange or a helping of cabbage.

As you can see, you don't need sweets, biscuits, cakes or soft drinks. Although these are often high in calories, and pregnant women probably need between 2500 and 3000 calories a day, they have little nutritional value. So if you feel the need for a snack at work, don't keep a drawer full of sweets or biscuits. Nibble on a bunch of grapes or a handful of raisins, even a raw carrot or a wholewheat crispbread.

Working in early pregnancy can be the most difficult time, for all the reasons mentioned earlier. You may be trying to keep your pregnancy secret, pretending that you are no different from usual, while all the time you are aware of the changes that are going on in your body. You may be struggling to cope with feelings of sickness or nausea, you may be rushing off to the loo at what seems like fifteen-minute intervals during the day. Above all, you may feel bone-tired, and collapse the minute you stagger in at night.

Your habits may have changed. You probably don't have the energy for socializing at this stage, you may not want to go to places where others are smoking and drinking. Sometimes you might even find yourself wondering if work is taking too much out of you, if you might not feel better if you were at home all day.

A technician who worked through three pregnancies told me: 'I have to admit the early days were dreadful. And the first time round I did wonder if I'd made the right decision to stay on at work. But financially we couldn't afford to have me at home all the time and I'm sure from talking to other mothers who didn't work that it can be even worse if you've got nothing to do all day but think about how sick and tired you are feeling.

'During the second pregnancy I felt just as awful at the beginning but I knew it was only a temporary stage. After twelve weeks or so I felt fine and I really enjoyed the rest of the pregnancy. And the pattern was the same in the third. By this time our financial situation was better and I could have stopped work if I'd wanted to. But normally I enjoy work and I knew things would soon get better.

'I just marked the date on the calendar when I expected to feel as right as rain and told myself there was light at the end of the tunnel.'

4
The new you

Is the fuller figure in fashion this year?

In one of the newspaper offices where I once worked there was a pretty blonde secretary who always looked immaculate from the tips of her polished nails to the soles of her stiletto shoes. She looked smart, she looked sexy, she looked efficient. And then she got pregnant.

Those of us who expected her to slide gracefully into the accepted uniform of tent-like pinafore dresses and low heels should have known better. Of course, she had to give up wearing the wide belts that accentuated her waist but she simply left her straight skirts unbuttoned, swapped her own white silk blouses for her husband's cotton shirts and wore them outside rather than tucked in. And she stuck to her stilettoes right to the last.

Some years later when I got pregnant and was faced with the problem of what to wear to work, I remembered her, and I decided to copy her, not in the exact manner of her dress, but in her attitude to what she wore. What Suzie had was her own particular style, and it was that style she managed to retain through her pregnancy.

It may seem frivolous in a book about pregnancy and work to devote a whole chapter to clothes and the way you look, but psychologists have shown that these things can affect your work performance and your self-confidence. Whether your job involves wearing a uniform or not, you probably have two wardrobes, work clothes and weekend clothes. Just as men put on overalls or a business suit and switch on their work self, so women also have clothes which signal work.

Choosing clothes
The right clothes can not only put you in the right frame of mind for work, but they can also influence other people's attitudes towards you. If your job involves meeting the public, dealing with clients or being on show in any way, then your choice of clothes is far more limited than if you have a backroom job where no one cares whether you turn up in designer dresses or jeans.

None of this changes when you are pregnant, but finding pregnancy clothes which echo the clothes you usually wear is not always easy.

If you have the kind of job where casual clothes are acceptable, then you should not have too many problems. Even in the space of five years, things have changed. When I was pregnant with my daughter it was not easy to find tracksuits, T-shirts, sweaters or trousers made for pregnant women. Now these things are far more easily available. If you cannot find them in the shops locally, try mail order.

Mothercare, for instance, sell pull-on trousers with drawstring waists, jumpers, dungarees and sweatshirts in the winter, T-shirts and shorts in the summer. Blooming Marvellous is a mail order company which also sells dungarees, jumpsuits and sweatshirts with witty slogans, as well as track suits, T-shirts and shorts.

On the other hand, if you need to look smart for work, you may find it hard to get away from the traditional mumsy tent dresses without spending a lot of money. Many women feel it is not worth spending a lot on outfits which will only be worn for a few months. Others feel that if they will enjoy wearing the clothes, they are worth the investment. Either way, it is worth noting a couple of points. First of all, you may end up wearing your pregnancy clothes for longer than you think. It is a rare woman who can wriggle back into her size 10 jeans a week after giving birth! This being the case, it is a good idea to look out for tops and dresses which have front fastenings if you are going to breastfeed. Secondly, if you spend more on a classic outfit that is better made and in a style you actually like, you could find that it will see you happily through any subsequent pregnancies, rather than having to buy a new lot of cheaper clothes each time.

Unless you are very unlucky you should be able to find some aspect of the current fashions which can be adapted to your changing state. Drop-waisted dresses and baggy overshirts are two examples from the fashions of the past few years.

Many of the women I interviewed for this book admitted they got by without buying many clothes actually designed for pregnant women. One public relations consultant told me: 'I didn't buy a single maternity outfit. I was fortunate that I didn't get vast, so I was able to buy loose styles in a larger size than usual. I did look at some stylish maternity clothes, but decided I didn't want to spend £80 on a dress I didn't really like anyway.'

A buyer for a chain store chose four patterns from the Vogue maternity range and made them herself. She said: 'By choosing my own materials I felt I was putting my own stamp on what I wore, rather than having to conform to someone else's idea of what pregnant women should look like.' If you don't have the talent, or the time, to sew your own, it might be worth finding a local dressmaker and paying her. It could still work out cheaper in the long run.

The Laura Ashley shops are usually worth investigating. Despite the flowery image, they also do smart plain pinafores and dresses. However, if your budget is not too tight and you definitely need stylish clothes to see you through a working pregnancy, then a trip to one of the more exclusive maternity wear boutiques in London or other large cities might pay off. Even the Mothercare catalogue now features a clutch of more sophisticated day designs—an indication that there is a demand for smart clothes for working pregnant women.

Borrowing or hiring clothes

During my first working pregnancy, when I was office rather than home based, I found I needed more outfits than I did second time round. I adapted some ordinary fashions, bought some maternity ones and swallowed my pride and borrowed things from friends..

I was lucky because I knew other women with similar tastes and jobs, not to mention similar shapes, who had already been pregnant and had clothes sitting idle in the back of their wardrobes. It certainly introduced variety in a way I could not otherwise have afforded. Even if you do not have girl-friends you can beg, borrow or steal from, you could try contacting former working mums through an ad on the noticeboard in your local baby clinic or your doctor's surgery.

Some local branches of the National Childbirth Trust run Rent-a-tent schemes, where, for a reasonable sum, you can borrow outfits for as long as you need them. If you do not know the number of your local branch, you can get it from the headquarters in London.

Or there might be a branch of Bumpsadaisy near you. Bumpsadaisy was set up by Penny Swithinbank when she was expecting her third child and was feeling very bored with her own maternity clothes. She says: 'I longed for something different, but couldn't justify spending a lot of money on something which would be worn for only a short time. The idea of Bumpsadaisy maternity hire was most appealing!'

Penny says she is only too well aware of the difficulties of buying clothes when you are pregnant. 'Mistakes are easily made, the clothes are not what you imagined you wanted and you're too tired to tramp all the shops to find just what you want.'

Bumpsadaisy offers a range of clothes to hire, from tracksuits to dresses, dungarees to evening wear. Penny says that for the price of one expensive dress you could have a different outfit every week for five months.

However pleased you are about your pregnancy, and however keen you are to announce your state to the world, it is best to leave shopping for clothes for as long as possible, particularly if you are planning to work late in pregnancy. After all, it is not just your stomach that will grow. Many women put on weight all over, particularly on their bottoms and thighs, not to mention their busts. The only time I ever have a cleavage is when I am pregnant. Last time I went from a 36A to a 38D!

Apart from this, whether you have a couple of pregnancy outfits or half a dozen or more, one thing is certain: you will be sick to death of them after a few months. The longer you can delay the move into your pregnancy wardrobe the better.

Clothes for summer and winter

When you do go shopping for pregnancy clothes, there are a few factors it is worth bearing in mind. The first is that when you are pregnant you have your own form of central heating and you probably will not feel as chilly as other mortals. Man-made fibres can be sticky and you may prefer to look for natural fabrics like silks or cottons. On the other hand, you will want some degree of crease resistance, particularly if you have to travel to work, and you will not want to fuss with clothes that need a lot of careful hand-washing or fiddly ironing. If you are out at work all day you will want to minimize your household chores as much as possible.

There are advantages and disadvantages to both summer and winter pregnancies. Having worked through one of each I think, on balance, I prefer coping with the heat of a summer rather than the cold and wet of a winter. In summer, you do not have to worry about finding a coat or mac that will cover the bump. For my winter working pregnancy, someone lent me a cape which solved the problem, looked reasonably stylish and saved me quite a bit of money.

Another girlfriend bought an ancient fur coat at a charity shop and turned it into a jacket for much less than the price of a new one. She said that after she had had the baby she didn't care if she never wore it again. It had served its purpose and cost next to nothing.

In winter, too, there is the problem of what to wear on your legs. Maternity tights do not usually come in the most flattering styles and colours. Like many women, I just bought the biggest size of ordinary tights I could find for as long as I could get away with it. Towards the end of pregnancy, even things you once took for granted become almost impossible. I found it hard to reach my toes and there were mornings when I had to get my husband to help me put my tights on! It was hilarious at the time, but with hindsight it was probably good training for him. He has no excuse for not helping our daughter now, when she gets her tights inside out or back to front.

If you have the kind of job where you can wear socks under trousers, you will not have this problem. If you do have to wear skirts, though, don't be tempted by hold-up stockings. They are not a good idea because the elastic tops have to be firm to work, and so they may constrict the blood flow in your legs and cause varicose veins. For the same reason, you should also avoid boots, jeans or girdles that are skin-tight.

Shoes

Shoes can turn out to be an unexpected extra expense. During pregnancy most of the ligaments in the body soften because the softening of the ligaments in the pelvis make it easier for the baby to be born. The ligaments of your feet are no exception. Well-fitting shoes are important but towards the end of pregnancy you may find that the shoes you have no longer fit. I needed a size 6 instead of my normal size 5. Other women find they need a broader fitting. Doctors generally advise against very high heels which throw your weight forward on to the balls of your feet and many women find they cannot wear these kind of shoes in pregnancy anyway. Your balance and posture does change and it is best to follow the dictates of your body rather than fashion. On the other hand, some women can wear high heels right to the end of their pregnancy with no difficulty. Some enjoy the fact that their feet, at least, look sexy!

Underwear

Certainly most of the underwear designed for pregnant women is anything but sexy. Take bras, for instance. Your breasts start to change from the very beginning of your pregnancy so you need bras which give good support. It is not only your cup size which will change, but the measurements underneath your breasts, around your rib cage. By the end of pregnancy your rib cage may be three to four inches bigger.

The bras designed for pregnant women usually have wide straps to take the extra weight, a wide band under the cups, and either lacing or a series of hooks at the back to allow for rib cage expansion. They almost invariably come in clinical white and look more like straight jackets than lingerie. Most of them double up as nursing bras and have front openings for breastfeeding. The prettiest of all is made by Anita in a lacy design, but even this is nothing to get madly excited about. As for most maternity knickers, with their stretch front panels to accommodate the bump, they reminded me of the kind of thing my grandmother used to wear. However, Mothercare have now introduced some bikini styles that are a vast improvement.

I suspect I am not the only woman who feels better when she is wearing pretty undies. I made a decision fairly early on in pregnancy that I would avoid the maternity underwear for as long as possible. I did not mind buying two extra bras in a bigger size than usual because they made me feel glamorous rather than functional. I stuck to bikini briefs for as long as they would cling under the bump and then I shopped around for the largest sized French knickers that would go over it.

Other women take the view that what the eye doesn't see the heart doesn't grieve over, and prefer to spend money on their outer, not their underwear. One girlfriend cold-dyed her maternity undies navy. She said they felt slightly more wicked, even if they didn't really look that way.

Changes to eyes, skin and hair

Clothes can help you look good and feel good, and that, in turn, can help you work better. But clothes are only part of the picture. Pregnancy does not only alter your vital statistics, it can also affect your hair, your skin, your teeth, even your eyes. It can come as quite a shock to some contact lens wearers to discover that their lenses are no longer as comfortable as they used to be. This can happen if, during pregnancy, extra fluid is retained in the body and produces a very slight change in the shape of the eyeball itself.

If this happens to you there is little you can do about it. Things will return to normal after the baby is born, and in the meantime, you can take advantage of the better, brighter and somewhat cheaper range of spectacles now available.

For some women, pregnancy is better than a series of expensive beauty treatments. Their skin glows and their hair shines. For others, it has quite the opposite result. The hormones produced in pregnancy affect every woman's skin differently. If your skin was greasy, as mine was, you may develop dry patches. If you had dry skin, the opposite may occur. I also discovered darker patches of skin across my forehead. The technical term for this kind of pigmentation is chloasma, but it is also called the mask of pregnancy. It is made worse by exposure to sunlight – mine developed after a holiday sunning myself in Portugal.

If your skin does change, you may need to experiment with a different beauty routine. Try to buy small or sample sizes of creams and cosmetics as you will probably find your skin goes back to normal after the baby is born. If your skin is particularly dry, it may feel itchy. Itchy skin is quite a common occurrence in pregnancy, and there is one theory that it may be caused by a lack of vitamins in the B group. However, if you are already eating a balanced diet, the best thing is to use lashings of oil or cream. You don't need to use expensive concoctions: a drop of baby oil in the bath or baby lotion rubbed on afterwards can be just as effective.

Choosing the best hairstyle

Many of the pregnancy books suggest that now is the time to try a new hairstyle. I personally doubt it. Whether your hair is thicker and more lustrous than usual (don't be too smug if it is – like me, you could find it falling out in handfuls after the birth) or even more unruly, you have probably got enough to cope with getting used to a new shape without the trauma of getting used to a new hairstyle as well.

You may think that it seems a good idea to have highlights, or a perm that can simply be finger-dried, but during pregnancy hair often reacts differently to tints and perms so you would be better advised to wait until about six months after the baby is born.

On the other hand, if you have very long hair that takes ages to wash and dry, or a style that needs attention every day to look good, you may want to think again. It is no fun bending over a bath or handbasin to wash your hair when you are the size of an elephant, and when all you want most in the world is another half hour in bed, it is awful having to drag yourself up to spend the time crimping in front of the mirror.

Don't rush into anything, however. Better a hairstyle you know how to manage than a new one that looks wonderful when you step out of the hairdresser's, yet makes you look as if you have been dragged through a hedge backwards after one night's sleep.

Pamper yourself sometimes
If you do want to treat yourself – and now is the time for a little pampering – consider having a facial or a manicure. An ante-natal teacher once remarked that she could always tell the first-time-mums in her classes even before she checked her records. They were the only ones who wore nail varnish. This is not a bad idea for all mums-to-be. Once the baby has arrived and you are knee-deep in nappies and baby clothes, painting your nails will not be very high on your list of priorities.

Less frivolous, but more useful, might be to book yourself a visit with a chiropodist. Many women do not realize that they are entitled to free chiropody as well as free prescriptions and dental treatment while they are pregnant. If you have problems getting chiropody treatment on the NHS (many GPs are unaware of this entitlement), contact the chiropody department of your local health authority or local community clinic.

Some women claim that a little indulgence can buck you up more than buying expensive maternity clothes. One suggestion is to have a Micheline Arcier aromatherapy massage for pregnant women with vitaminized tangerine oil. It is a soothing way to release tension and as a sideline you also receive advice on diet during pregnancy. It is not cheap. When I was told about it, an initial one-hour massage (plus half an hour consultation) cost £27, and subsequent massages cost £18 each.

During my first pregnancy I spent a weekend at a health farm. This was not cheap either, but it was worth every penny. I made sure they knew I was pregnant and although I had to skip the sauna it was nice being able to eat anything while everyone else sipped hot water or fruit juice, and I enjoyed making full use of the pool, having a facial and massage and generally being able to relax.

Looking after your teeth
There used to be an old wives' tale that said you lost a tooth for

every baby. It was thought that because the growing baby needs calcium, it took this from your teeth. In fact, although the baby does need calcium, it does not get it from your teeth and this is not the reason why pregnant women are particularly vulnerable to dental decay.

What happens is that, as a result of the pregnancy hormones in your blood, your gums become softer and more liable to inflammation and diseases. It is particularly important to clean your teeth properly during pregnancy. Make sure that there are no food particles trapped between them, and no build-up of plaque. If you do not already do so, get into the habit of keeping a toothbrush and toothpaste at work and brushing regularly after eating anything. However hard-pressed you are for time in the mornings and however tired you feel at night, don't skimp on your dental routine.

Making the effort to feel good

Taking care of your appearance during a working pregnancy, is not just a matter of vanity. It is not always easy to find the right kind of clothes or to make enough time for a regular beauty routine. In the early days you may be feeling so rotten that you don't care what you look like, or so tired that you can't be bothered to make the effort. Later on, you may feel so cumbersome that the last thing you want to do is to wash your hair or spend your lunch hour trying to find a dress that looks like a dress and not a circus big top. But it is worth making the effort. I worked at home for most of my second pregnancy and found it was only too easy not to bother too much about the way I looked. I wore clothes left over from the time before, plus anything else that fitted, and for a while I could not understand why I felt so fed-up and lethargic. It seemed a ridiculous extravagance to go out and buy anything new, and since I wasn't looking remotely like a fashion plate, it seemed crazy to bother much about make-up or whether my hair needed cutting.

Then a girlfriend came round and jolted me out of it. She practically ordered me to go out and spend some money on myself and she was right. With a couple of new outfits, plus some she lent me, I felt like a different person, and I began to behave like one too. I got more work done in less time and I felt far happier.

THE NEW YOU

An American psychologist has found that our facial expressions do not mirror our moods, they create them. When you frown, you tense your face, contract the muscles and cut the flow of blood to the brain. The result can be dysphoria, the opposite of euphoria. So you feel sad. When you smile, the action of the cheek muscles stop blood draining out of the brain and this makes you feel good.

Few of us can manage to go around all day with a smile glued to our faces, but I believe there are other things we can do to change our moods for the better. Making ourselves look good, in whatever way we can, is a positive step in the right direction. However wanted a pregnancy, it can be hard coming to terms with the fact that your waist now measures twice what it used to, that your slender ankles are swollen, that your English rose complexion is covered with spots. But if lashing out on an outrageously expensive outfit is going to make you feel fantastic – or even halfway presentable – then it will be worth every penny. And I believe that the better you feel, the better you will be, and the better you will be able to cope with your work.

Useful information
Mothercare: There are more than 200 Mothercare stores in the UK so there should be one within your reach. To find out where your nearest branch is, or if you have any other queries, you can phone the Customer Service Department at Mothercare's Head Office in Cherry Tree Road, Watford, Herts. Tel: 0923 31616. Calls are taken between 9 a.m. and 5 p.m. After 5 p.m. and at weekends, an automatic answering service will accept a message.

If you cannot get to one of the shops, or if you simply cannot face the hassle, Mothercare produce a catalogue and you can use this to order goods by post. The catalogues – which change twice yearly – are available in the stores and are also sent to anyone who has used the Mothercare-by-Post service within the previous six months. There is no permanent mailing list.

You can also order by telephone if you use an Access card, Visa card, Eurocard or Mastercard, or if you have one of Mothercare's own credit cards. If you don't like the goods when you get them, or if they don't fit, you will be able to get an exchange or a refund provided you return them within two weeks of receipt.

Although the Mothercare catalogue is pretty big (the one I have has 211 pages), only a relatively small section is devoted to the needs of the expectant mother, as opposed to babies and children. However, it does cover the basics, from casual clothes to a handful of smarter outfits, from underwear to nightwear, tights to toiletries.

Blooming Marvellous produce a catalogue completely devoted to maternity wear. It is available from PO Box 12F, Chessington, Surrey KT9 2LS. If you have any queries regarding the clothes or an order you can ring the company on 01-391 4119 between 9.30 a.m. and 2.30 p.m. If you have an Access or Barclaycard, you can telephone your order on 01-397 5954. If you are not completely satisfied with your purchase, the company guarantees to exchange it or refund your money in full provided the clothes are returned unworn within seven days. Catalogues and order forms can also be obtained by telephoning 01-391 4822.

If you are buying clothes by post, it is often hard to know which size to choose, particularly when you are pregnant. Both catalogues give some advice. Mothercare have their own sizing system. For dresses, tops, nighties and slips 01 fits bust 33 to 37 inches, 02 fits bust 38 to 41 inches and anything marked 'one size' fits bust 33 to 41 inches. Dungarees, trousers and jumpsuits are either 01 (hips 34-38 inches) or 02 (hips 39-43 inches) but jeans are 00 (34-36 inches), 01 (hips 37-39 inches) or 02 (hips 40-43 inches).

Most of the Blooming Marvellous clothes come in standard British sizes 10, 12, 14 and 16, and they suggest you quote your pre-pregnant size on the order form as the outfits have been designed to flatter your new figure. Helpfully, they add that their dress lengths are approximately 45 inches and trouser and dungarees have an inside leg measurement of approximately 33 inches.

Both catalogues give clear instructions on how to measure yourself to find an accurate bra size. The Mothercare bras stop at a D cup, but one of the Blooming Marvellous styles goes up to E.

Laura Ashley have ten shops in London and about forty-nine others (not counting the home decorating shops) dotted about the country from Bath to Edinburgh. They also run a mail order service.

A selected number of clothes are featured in the Laura Ashley magazines, which can be bought at newsagents or direct from the company. Some of the outfits could be worn during pregnancy. Two examples were a flower print, high-waisted dress and a pinafore in navy windowpane check. Dresses and blouses come in conventional 10, 12, 14, 16 sizes; T-shirts and jumpers are either one size, or S, M, L.

If you have an Access or Visa card you can order by telephone at any time, using the answerphone service on 0686 24842. If the clothes do not fit, or do not come up to your expectations in any way you can return them within fourteen days and you will get a refund.

For information about an order or about the Mail Order Service, contact Mail Order Customer Services, Laura Ashley Ltd, Box 5, Carno, Powys, Wales SY17 5LQ, or telephone 0686 24684 from Monday to Friday, between 9 a.m. to 5 p.m.

For general inquiries or complaints about the service, contact Customer Services, Laura Ashley Ltd, Braywick House, Braywick Road, Maidenhead, Berkshire, or telephone 0628 39151, from Monday to Friday between 9 a.m. and 5 p.m.

Aromatherapy massage for pregnant women. For a Micheline Arcier trained therapist, ring or visit the salon at 7 William Street, London SW1X 9HL. Tel: 01-235 3545.

5
Getting the balance right

If you are holding down a full-time job *and* running a home, you may well feel you have neither the time nor the energy to fit in any form of exercise as well. Even so, it is important to keep fit during pregnancy and to prepare yourself for the labour to come. It is also a good idea to make some time for yourself each day, when you concentrate on your own pleasure or relaxation and get in touch with the needs of your body.

Most of us suffer stress in some form or another and exercise is one way of alleviating stress. Ironically enough, if you feel under pressure trying to balance the demands of work, home and pregnancy, then taking some time for regular exercise may give you more energy to cope with everything else in your life, rather than finishing you off altogether. It is not always easy to get things into perspective, but if you ever needed to learn the lesson that no one can really be Superwoman, now is the time.

After all, who but you will know whether the oven got cleaned this week or not? And a round of wholemeal cheese and tomato sandwiches which can be prepared in a minute, are just as nutritious as a chop and two veg, which take much longer to cook.

What kind of exercise?

Finding the time is one thing. Choosing the right kind of exercise is another. Perhaps you already do some kind of sport or keep-fit exercise. Should you continue?

These days the medical profession is far less cautious in its advice to pregnant women than it used to be. Generally speaking, provided you are in good health and you do not have a history of miscarriage or premature labour, there is no reason why you should not continue most sports or exercise routines.

Women can, and do, continue to play badminton and go cycling. However, most doctors advise against sports which are especially vigorous or dangerous, such as horse riding, marathon running, or ski-ing. And whatever form of exercise you choose, you should never go on until you feel exhausted and you should always stop if you feel any pain.

If sport is not part of your life and you have no established exercise plan, now is not the time to embark upon anything particularly demanding. But this does not mean that all forms of physical activity must be ruled out. Professor Geoffrey Chamberlain suggests: 'If you have not embarked on a keep-fit programme of one sort or another then a little gentle exercise such as walking a mile or so each day or swimming twice a week would be very beneficial.'

Swimming can be particularly relaxing, especially in later pregnancy when the illusion of weightlessness is almost miraculous. Thankfully, these days no one is prudish about the sight of a pregnant woman in a swimsuit, or even a bikini, which many women find preferable to the one-pieces on the market. Gone are the days when you took to the water in a swimsuit with voluminous skirts: the modern versions in stretch fabrics are smarter and much more fun.

Swimming is actually one of the best all-round forms of exercise, but it has some effects which are particularly relevant for pregnant women. If you practise your breaststroke you will also be strengthening your thigh muscles, a useful preparation for labour and delivery.

Yoga

Yoga is another form of exercise which can be taken up or continued during pregnancy. Sophy Hoare, who teaches yoga to pregnant women and who herself practised yoga through all her four pregnancies, is convinced of the benefits. She says: 'It is even more important to take some form of exercise during pregnancy than it is normally, since extra demands are made on the body from the very beginning. Not only can yoga contribute to your well-being and that of the baby during pregnancy, but it will probably help you cope with the birth and help you get back to normal quicker during the post-natal period.'

To the working women who reply that they already seem to be rushing around so much they surely do not need any more exercise, she says: 'You may feel you are rushing about a lot, but unless you are actually involved with some form of manual labour it is not the same kind of thing as exercise at all. Many women have fairly sedentary jobs. And something like yoga can give you extra energy. When you are tense because you feel under pressure you are using muscles to create that state. By teaching you how to loosen those muscles, you no longer waste that energy.

'Pregnancy is not the right time to take up anything very strenuous and that is why yoga is so good, particularly the form of yoga I teach, Iyengar yoga, which is geared towards strengthening the body, rather than concentrating on meditation.'

Exercises for pregnancy

If most of your pregnancy takes place through the winter months you may not feel like going out for walks or making an expedition to yoga classes or to the local swimming pool. You may prefer an exercise programme that can be carried on in your own home. In any case, it is a good idea to try some of the exercises that are good for pregnant women since many of them help to tone up the abdominal muscles, and others can be a help with so many of the minor complaints of pregnancy, such as backache, cramps, varicose veins, sleeplessness, tiredness, and nausea.

The beauty of the first two exercises is that they can be done anywhere. This makes them especially useful for working women who are short of spare time.

It is particularly important to exercise the muscles of the pelvic floor. These muscles support everything within the pelvic cavity, including the uterus, the bladder and the rectum. During the pregnancy, these muscle layers are under extra stress. If you are not aware of these muscles, the best way to discover how they work is to sit on the loo and try to stop halfway through urinating.

The idea is to exercise and strengthen the pelvic floor muscles gradually. One way of doing this is to imagine they represent a lift. You tighten the muscles as if the lift was going to the first floor, and hold it there. Then you tighten further as you go up to the second floor, and hold it there. If possible you go up a third or even a fourth floor. Finally, you come back down again, but gradually rather than in one big rush. Finish off with a toning movement, a slight lift up to the mezzanine floor.

You need to practice this one often. I used to do it standing on the platform waiting for my tube at Charing Cross, whenever I dialled a number on the phone, waiting for the kettle to boil.

The next exercise discourages varicose veins by stimulating the flow of blood back to the heart. If you work sitting down, you can practise it at any time. Keep your knees slightly apart and your legs still, lift one foot off the ground and rotate it, or draw letters with it. Then repeat with the other foot (Figure 1).

Avoiding aches and pains

Correct posture is important when you are pregnant, particularly if your job involves a lot of standing. As your bump gets bigger and heavier, you tend to throw back your shoulders and stick your bottom out. You take your weight on your heels and your back becomes hollowed, all of which can lead to low backache. Try to tuck your bottom in and relax your shoulders. Imagine you are a puppet with a string pulling you up straight from the top of your head.

If you have to be on your feet a lot, remember that walking is better than standing. If you have to stand, at least exercise your

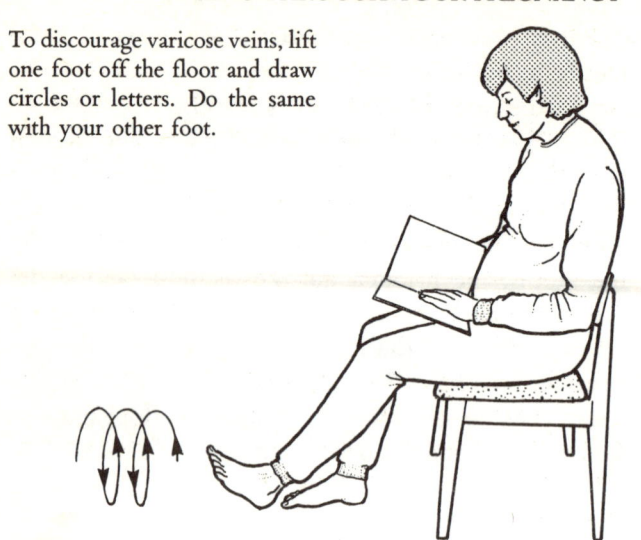

To discourage varicose veins, lift one foot off the floor and draw circles or letters. Do the same with your other foot.

Figure 1

feet, like a guardsman on parade. Flex and unflex your toes, shift your weight from one foot to the other. Go up on to the balls of your feet and down again.

If most of your working day is spent sitting at a desk, make sure your spine has enough support. You may find it helpful to put a small cushion in the small of your back.

One of the biggest complaints from the office workers who took part in the survey for this book was about office chairs. Don't suffer in silence. There may well be a more comfortable chair somewhere in the building. Take heart from the secretary who eventually got her boss to do a swap.

If you do a lot of typing you may find you suffer from upper backaches. The shoulder-roll exercise can help. Still sitting at your desk rest your fingertips on your shoulders and circle backwards with your elbows as if your arms were wings. Headaches can be another problem, often caused by tension in the neck and shoulders. Sit comfortably but keep your back straight. Drop your head forward and clasp your hands together behind your head. Gently bring your chin down towards your breastbone, drop your shoulders and breathe deeply. Hold this for a few seconds then bring your head up slowly.

Many women have jobs which involve bending and lifting. The

key thing to remember is to use your knees, not your back. Bend your knees and get right down to the load, rather than stooping over and using your spine like a crane. At home, kneel or squat when you are working low down. I found the most comfortable way of washing the kitchen floor was to forget the sponge-headed mop and get down on all fours in the old fashioned way. In fact, getting down on all fours is a good way of taking the weight of the baby off your spine and it can help if you have backache, although, unfortunately, the number of jobs you can do in this position is limited!

Rocking the pelvis can also help relieve low backache. One way of doing this is an exercise nicknamed the angry cat. Go down on all fours. Keep the small of your back flat and without moving your elbows or knees tighten your stomach muscles and arch your lower back. Hold this position for a few seconds then relax, but do not let your back hollow. Repeat this sequence about ten times (Figure 2).

Get down on all fours and — very important — keep the small of your back flat.

Without moving your elbows or knees, tighten your stomach muscles and arch your lower back. Hold this position for a few seconds then relax.

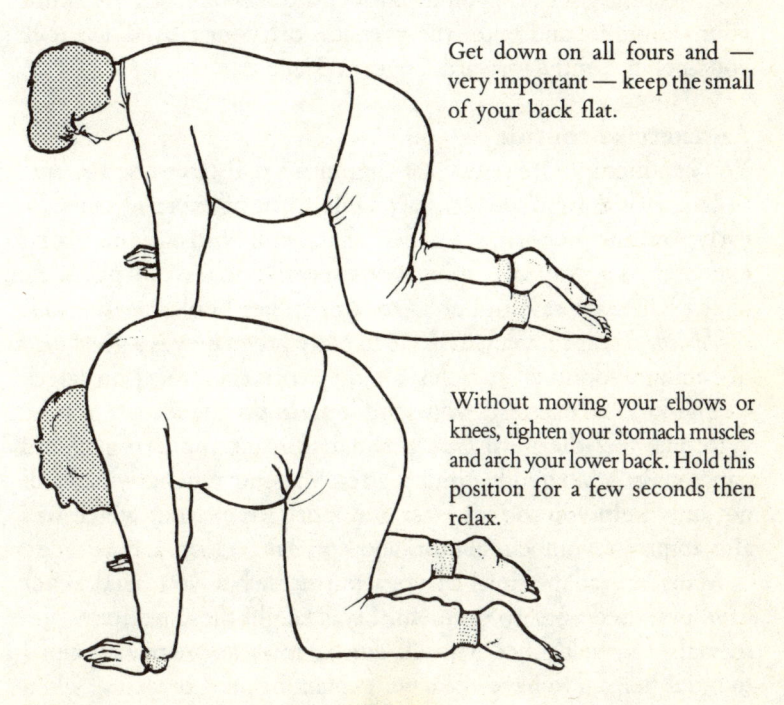

Figure 2

You can also practise pelvic rocking by lying on a flat surface such as the floor or a firm bed, with your knees bent and your feet flat. Pull your tummy muscles in and press the cheeks of your bottom together while you breathe out through your mouth. Then release the muscles as you gently rock your pelvis forward and breathe in through your nose. Don't make the sequence too hurried or jerky, or the movement too exaggerated, and repeat for as long as you feel comfortable.

Pelvic rocking and circling are useful exercises which can also help during labour. My daughter decided to arrive in a face-up position rather than the more conventional face-down one, and I had the typical backache labour associated with babies in posterior positions. As a result, I spent most of the time on all fours waggling my bottom around, and it did help.

Kneel on the floor with your arms folded on the seat of a stool or chair, then circle your pelvis round to the left or the right. Repeat ten times in both directions. Or try sitting astride a kitchen chair resting your arms on a pillow on the chair-back. This lifts your shoulders and takes the pressure off your ribs. Then rock your pelvis gently forward (Figures 3 and 4).

An exercise routine

You can incorporate pelvic rocking into a daily exercise routine. In fact, it is a good idea to start some form of exercise schedule early on in pregnancy, rather than simply using particular exercises as a way of coping with specific aches and pains. As Sheila Kitzinger says of pelvic rocking in her book *Pregnancy and Childbirth*, 'This movement done in early pregnancy is a good way of toning abdominal muscles for the work they must do later.'

The kind of exercises you should do in pregnancy are not the vigorous, feel-the-burn type popular in many modern gym and dance classes, but gentle, toning, stretching movements which will not only help you to feel fitter and more supple, but which will also improve your circulation and combat tension and fatigue.

Many are adaptations of yoga postures, but you need never have practised yoga to do them. I was taught these exercises at a special class held once a week during my last pregnancy and I found it helpful to have a teacher explaining and correcting when necessary, though if you cannot find such a class in your area there is no reason why you cannot follow the programme by yourself at home. However, if you have a chronic back problem or if you have had any complications in this or previous pregnancies, such as a history of miscarriage or a cervical stitch, check with your doctor first.

Some doctors suggest it is best to wait until after the twelfth week before you embark on the exercises unless you are already used to yoga or working out. The sooner you start after that the better, although it is never too late to gain some benefit.

Circling your pelvis round to the left and right can help relieve backache in labour.

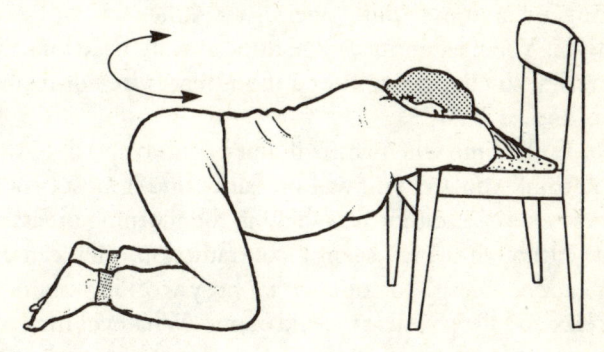

Figure 3

Figure 4

Sitting in this position lifts your shoulders and takes the pressure off your ribs. Gently rock your pelvis back and forth.

Getting started

Take it easy at first, trying out just a few examples and gradually building up as your body gets used to the positions. As you loosen up and lose your stiffness, the exercises will feel more comfortable, but if individual ones continue to feel wrong for you, leave them out. Always listen to what your body is telling you. Remember that this is not some kind of competition. This should ultimately be a pleasurable experience, not a painful one. The idea is to go as far as you need to feel the stretch, then to hold that position, breathing deeply, before gently coming out of it.

Wear something loose that will not restrict your movements. A track suit or a loose shirt over your knickers are suitable alternatives. You need quite a large floor or wall space for some of the exercises, so choose a part of a room that is free of furniture, radiators and so on.

Try to find a time when you will not be interrupted. However tired you think you are, you will probably find it most beneficial to do these exercises either first thing in the morning or last thing at night. Although it may seem a contradiction, they can either give you added energy to cope with a busy working day or help you to relax and sleep well at the end of one. Whatever time of day you choose, it is best not to have a large meal beforehand.

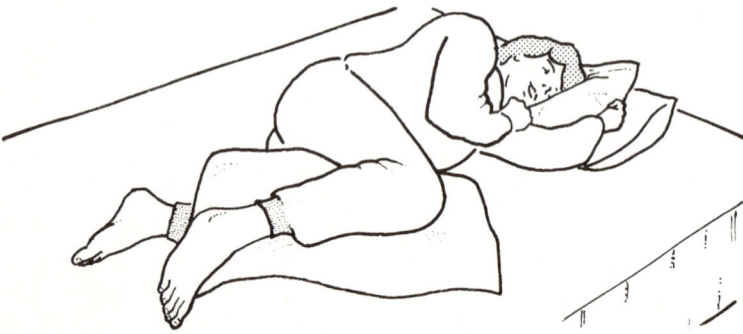

If you feel uncomfortable lying on your back this position is a very comfortable alternative.

Figure 5

Relax first

Start by sitting or lying quietly and relaxing completely. If you find it hard to relax, use the technique outlined in chapter 3.

Concentrate on your breathing, trying not to interrupt the flow.

A word of warning: some women find they cannot lie flat on their backs during pregnancy, particularly in the later months. The pressure of the uterus on the large blood vessels in your abdomen may slow down your circulation and make you feel faint. If you find this happens to you, or if you feel uncomfortable like this, roll over to your side, get on to all fours slowly and give up any exercise which involves lying on your back.

Another alternative is to lie on your side with your head resting on one pillow and your top knee bent and supported by another pillow, (Figure 5). This is also a good way to sleep if you have been finding it difficult to get comfortable at night. Or you could sit in the tailor position up against a wall so that your back is straight and supported. Cross your ankles, keep your feet as close to you as possible and let your knees drop as close to the ground as is comfortable (Figure 6).

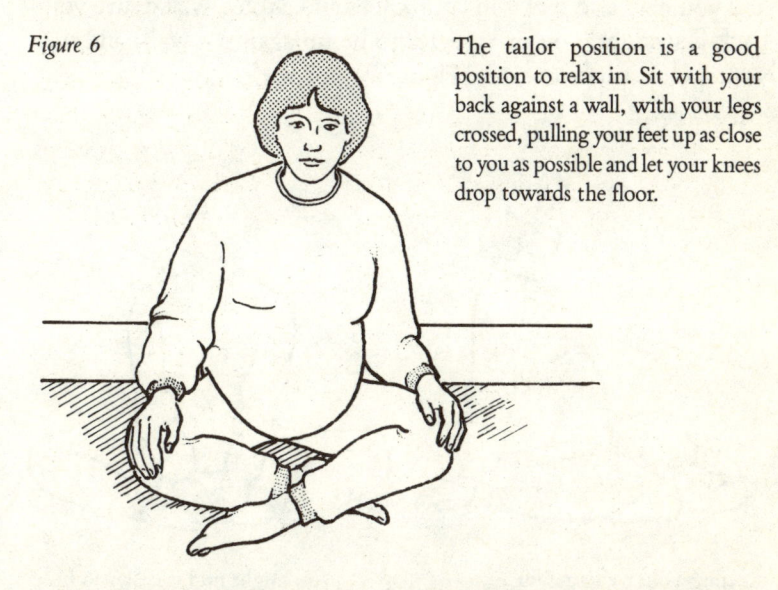

Figure 6

The tailor position is a good position to relax in. Sit with your back against a wall, with your legs crossed, pulling your feet up as close to you as possible and let your knees drop towards the floor.

Now begin to breathe in through your nose and out through your mouth. Breathe out fully, then pause until you feel the urge to breathe in again. Let your stomach draw in as you breathe out and expand as you breathe in. Concentrate on breathing out and let breathing in come naturally. Continue to pause between each breath. After a while, return to your normal breathing in and out through your nose. Now that you are relaxed and have cleared all distractions from your mind, you can begin the individual exercises. If you are lying down, roll over to your side and come up slowly into a sitting position.

Exercise 1

Sit up straight and bring the soles of your feet together as close to your body as possible. Put your hands behind you, with the palms down on the floor close to your bottom to help you keep your back straight, or else clasp your toes or ankles with your hands to help you lift your spine. Another tip is to put a rolled-up blanket under the back of your bottom. Now make up and down butterfly movements with your legs. You may not be able to let your knees drop to the floor at first, but you will get more supple with practice.

You should feel the stretch mainly in the groin and hip joints and you may also feel it in your knees and ankles. Make sure your back is straight (you may prefer to be up against a wall) and that your pelvis tilts forward, (Figure 7) not back.

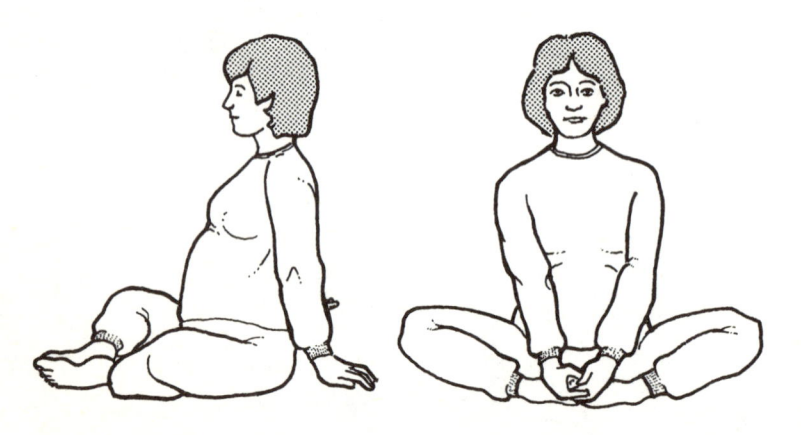

Keeping your back straight, bring the soles of your feet together as close to your body as you can. Raise and lower your knees as far as is comfortable without straining.

You might find it easier to keep your back straight during this exercise by clasping your toes or ankles. Raise and lower your knees as before.

Figure 7

GETTING THE BALANCE RIGHT

This exercise loosens the hip joints and the inner thigh muscles. It also tone up the pelvic floor muscles and improves the circulation of the blood to this area. It can be a very comfortable sitting position. Once you are used to it, you can use it to watch television or read.

If you are against a wall you can also interlock your fingers and stretch your arms out straight ahead of you, palms outwards. Keeping your arms stretched, inhale and raise them above your head. Do not hollow your back or push your ribs out. Hold for a moment, then exhale as you bring your arms down. Towards the end of pregnancy, this can feel wonderful as it opens up the body, giving the baby more space and you more room to breathe. You can do the same stretch standing with your feet about 2 feet apart, and this is worth trying if you are suffering from heartburn (Figure 8).

You can do this exercise standing or sitting against a wall. Interlock your fingers and stretch your arms straight out in front of you. Inhale and raise them above your head without hollowing your back or pushing your ribs out. Hold for a moment then exhale as you bring your arms down.

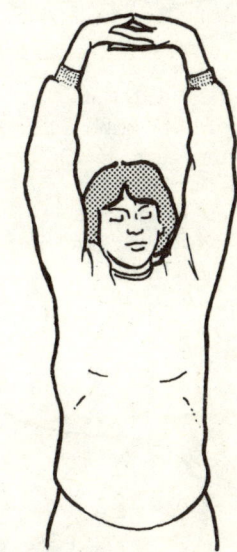

Figure 8

Exercise 2

Kneel on the floor with your knees as wide as possible, your ankles turned out and your toes pointing towards each other. Sit between your feet if you can, or else sit on your heels. Keep your back straight and bring your shoulder blades back and down to open your chest. Try to imagine a straight line running from your coccyx to the back of your head and move gently forwards, keeping your bottom down and your arms straight until your palms are flat on the floor. You should feel a stretch in your groin. Hold this position, breathing deeply, then slowly come up (Figures 9a and 9b).

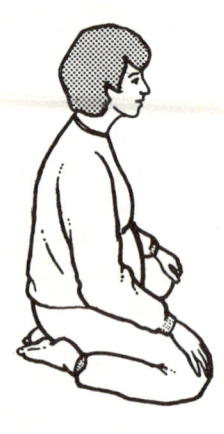

a Kneel on the floor with your knees as wide apart as possible, your ankles turned out, toes pointing towards each other. Sit between your feet or on your heels. Keep your back straight and move your shoulder blades back and down.

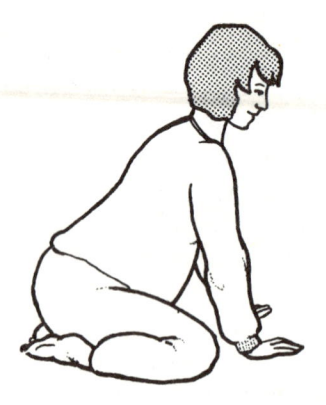

b Keeping your back straight, move gently forwards with your arms in front of you until your palms are flat on the floor. You should feel a stretch in your groin. Hold the position, breathe deeply, then slowly return to the sitting position.

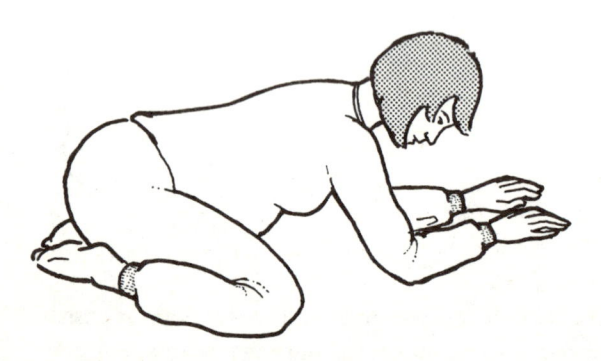

c If you do not feel a stretch when following **b**, do the same but move forward until you rest on your elbows, not bending your back.

Figure 9

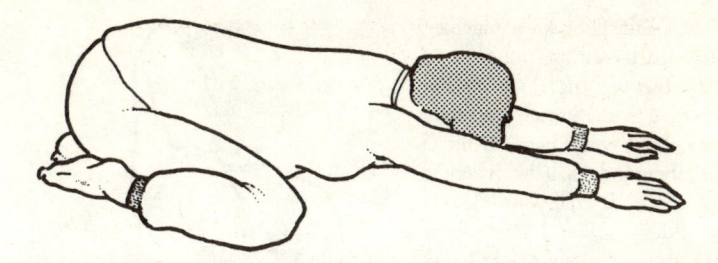

d If you still feel no stretch, slide your arms forward until you feel the pull in the groin, without too much force.

If you cannot feel a stretch, go further down to rest on your elbows, but make sure you do not bend your back. Get your partner to tell you if you are or not, or work in front of a mirror (Figures 9c and 9d).

If you still feel no stretch you can slide your arms forward and lie flat, but don't force it. The aim is to feel the pull in your groin, not to get as low as possible (Figure 9e).

This exercise is good for preventing and relieving back ache and it also relaxes your back, buttock and pelvic floor muscles. Small children often sleep in this position – my young son is still sometimes to be found head down and bottom up, out for the count. And the next sitting position is also one which children adopt naturally, sitting on the floor.

Exercise 3
Kneel up, knees together, feet apart, with the tops of your feet resting on the floor. Now sit down gently between your feet. If your knees or ankles are too stiff to manage this, put a pillow or folded blanket under your bottom. Stretch above your head with your right arm, bend the elbow and reach down behind your back as far as you can. Now stretch your left arm out sideways to shoulder height, bend your elbow and try to clasp your right hand with your left behind your back. Hold for a minute then reverse the position using opposite arms (Figure 10).

If you cannot make your fingers meet at first, use a handkerchief or scarf to hold on to. This exercise loosens the shoulders and the top of the spine.

Kneel on the floor, knees together, feet apart, resting the tops of your feet on the floor and sit between them. Stretch your right arm above your head, bend at the elbow and reach down behind your back. Stretch your left arm out sideways, bend your elbow and try to clasp your right hand. Hold this position for a minute and then reverse.

Figure 10

Exercise 4

Another exercise you can do while sitting between your feet involves leaning back.

Warning: Take this exercise very carefully. Do not go beyond your limit. If you feel any pain in your lower back, you must stop. In the beginning it is a good idea to put a pile of cushions or pillows behind you for support.

Tighten the muscles in your bottom then lean back on to your hands until you feel a stretch in your thighs. If you can feel a stretch, stop here (Figures 11a and 11b). If not, go back on to your elbows, keeping your bottom tight and your knees together (Figure 11c). If you are very supple and still feeling no stretch, you can go on to the next stage. Tighten your bottom, keep your knees together, lift your pubic bone and lie down flat. I used to be able to lie down with no problems, but getting up was harder. Uncurling my legs and rolling over seemed the safest way, if my partner or teacher was not there to lend a hand (Figure 11d).

This exercise is supposed to improve the circulation in your legs and strengthen your lower back. It may also help if you suffer from haemorrhoids, indigestion or heartburn.

Exercise 5

For this exercise you need a clear area of wall. Sit down sideways next to the wall so that the side of your bottom is touching it. Then swivel round so that, as you lie flat on your back, your bottom remains in touch with the wall and your legs are in the air. Bend your knees as if you were squatting and rest your feet against the wall. Lift your arms straight over your head (Figure 12a).

Now straighten your legs, keeping them together and hold this position for a few seconds until you are used to it (Figure 12b).

Let your legs drop apart, sliding down the wall as far as they can.

Warning: If you feel any pain in your lower back while doing this exercise, stop. At first, use plenty of pillows to support your back.

a Sit between your feet or on your ankles and tighten your buttock muscles.

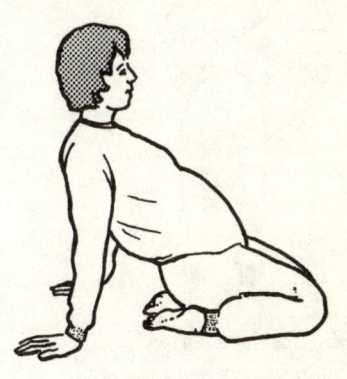

b Lean back onto the palms of your hands until you feel a stretch in your thighs.

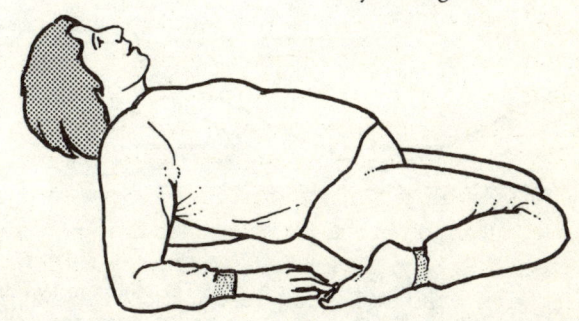

c If you do not feel a stretch in position **b** then, keeping your buttock muscles tight and your knees together, move back until you can rest on your elbows.

Figure 11

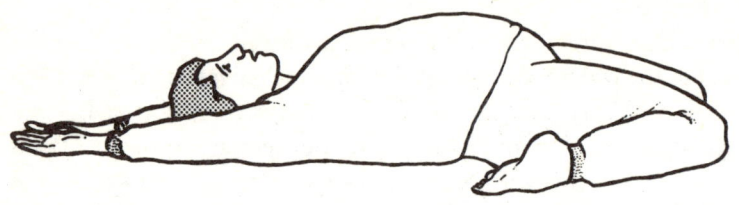

d If you still feel no stretch in position **c**, tighten your buttock muscles, keep your knees together, lift your pubic bone and lean right back. If nobody is there to help you up, it is best to uncurl your legs and roll over.

Figure 11

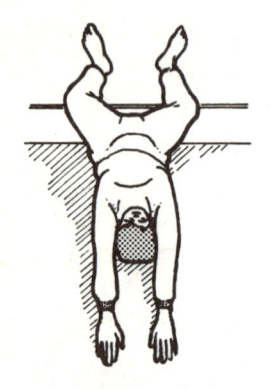

a Lying on the floor with your bottom against the skirting board, rest your feet on the wall as if you were squatting and lift your arms over your head.

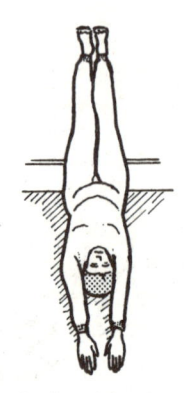

b From position **a**, slide your feet up the wall, keep your legs together and hold this position for a while.

c Then let your legs drop apart, sliding down the wall as far as they will go without straining too much, stretching your ankles as shown. Hold this position for a minute or two and breathe deeply.

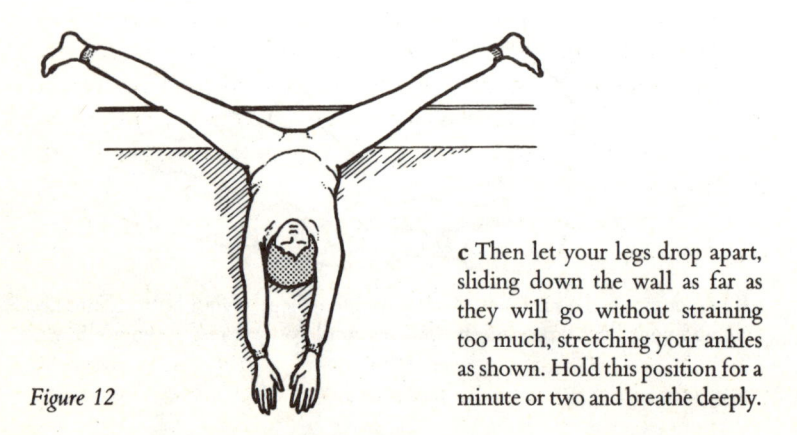

Figure 12

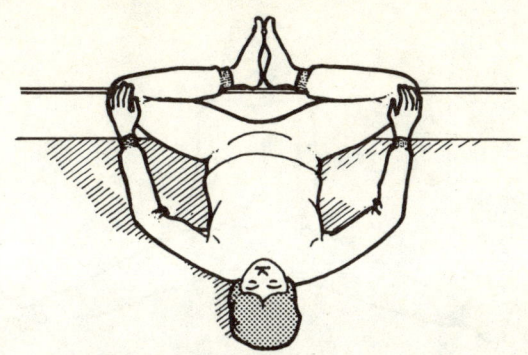

Figure 12

d If position **c** is too uncomfortable, try bending your knees, putting the soles of your feet together close to your bottom and gently push your knees towards the wall with your hands.

Stretch your ankles and point your toes in towards your body. You will feel the stretch in your inner thigh muscles and this might feel quite painful at first. Hold the position for a minute or so, breathing deeply. Massage the inner thigh muscles with your hands if it helps (Figure 12c).

If you find this position too uncomfortable, try bending your knees and putting the soles of your feet together, close to your bottom. Then gently push your knees towards the wall with your hands (Figure 12d).

The best way of getting up is to roll over slowly to your side, pause for a second or two, then go on to your hands and knees. *Warning:* Do not attempt this position if you feel dizzy lying on your back.

I used to find this exercise particularly good when I was feeling shattered after a hard day's work. Provided I could persuade my two-year-old daughter that lying on the ground with my legs in the air was not some kind of new game, a five or ten-minute session like this used to give me the energy to cope with her bath and bedtime routines.

It is also a good exercise to practise regularly if you suffer from varicose veins or haemorrhoids.

If you cannot lie on your back comfortably you can still stretch those inner thigh muscles by sitting on the floor with your legs as wide apart as possible. Keep your back straight and support yourself by leaning back slightly on to your hands. Flex your feet,

Figure 13

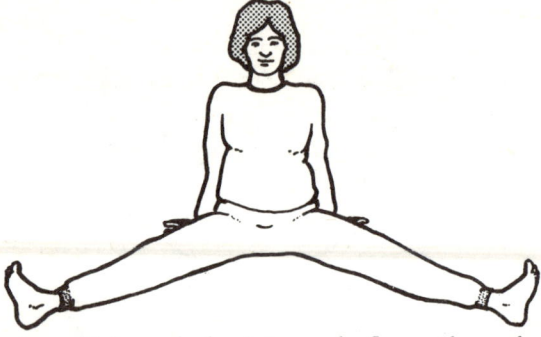

Stretch your inner thigh muscles by sitting on the floor with your legs as wide apart as possible, keeping your legs straight by supporting yourself with your arms as shown.

pointing your toes up and down (Figure 13).

Exercise 6

Sacro-iliac pain is hard to describe but pretty unmistakeable if you suffer from it. The pain occurs in the sacro-iliac joints and usually feels like a stabbing pain in the top of one of the cheeks of your bottom. It is different from the other kind of low backache you can get in pregnancy. I found the following exercise helpful for this pain.

Lie down on your back with your legs in front of you. Bend one knee and grasp that foot with the opposite hand. Bounce your bent knee gently towards the floor a few times, then swap over and repeat the movement using the other foot (Figure 14).

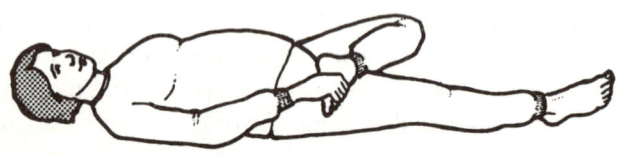

Lying on your back, bend your left knee and grasp the foot with your right hand. Bounce the knee gently towards the floor a few times. Repeat with the other leg.

Figure 14

Another exercise which can help to relieve or prevent backache or sacro-iliac pain is to lie flat on your back with your arms by your sides, then bend your knees and slide your feet back towards your bottom. Press your lower back into the floor, tighten the muscles in your bottom, and keeping them tight, breathe in. Lift your pelvis so that your back comes off the floor and hold the position for a second. Breathe out as you come down. You can repeat this three or four times (Figure 15a and 15b).

a Lie on the floor and adopt this position, pressing your lower back to the floor, tightening your buttock muscles and breathe in.

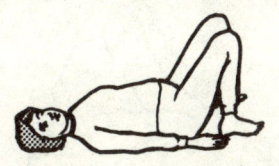

b Lift your bottom off the floor and hold the position for a second, then breathe out as you lower yourself back to the floor. Repeat three or four times.

Figure 15

Exercise 7

In recent years many advocates of natural childbirth have argued that the most natural way to give birth is in a squatting position. Even if you have no desire to deliver your baby this way, squatting during pregnancy has a number of advantages.

It improves the circulation to the whole pelvic area, so it is good for your baby. It opens up your pelvis and tones your back, bottom and pelvic floor muscles. It can help to ease backache and constipation. Having said all that, it can be very difficult to do at first.

Although it is a natural way to rest and a position which young children adopt frequently and effortlessly, most of us have lost the ability by the time we are adult. Practise by standing with your feet about hip-width apart and your feet parallel, toes forward rather than pointing sideways. Keeping your back in a straight line and your feet flat, squat down (Figure 16a).

If you are anything like me, you will already have lost your balance, but there are a few ways of making the process easier. Try placing a small cushion or book under your heels (Figure 16b). Hold on to a door handle or the side of a heavy sofa for support. Place a few large books under your bottom – you can reduce the pile as you get more proficient (Figure 16c). Try squatting against a wall.

These are the exercises I found most useful when I was pregnant, although they were not all easy at first. You do not have to do all of them. Experiment to find out which you enjoy most.

a Stand with feet hip-width apart, feet parallel, keep your back straight and then squat down.

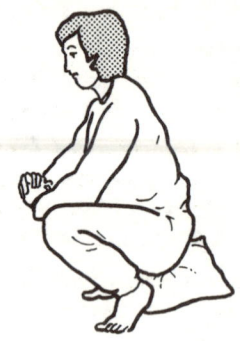

b Putting a cushion under your heels can help you squat if you lose your balance doing **a**.

Figure 16

Most of the pregnancy handbooks offer variations of some of these positions as well as exercises of their own. It should not be too difficult to work out your own routine. Always allow yourself time to rest and relax completely at the end of a session.

c A book can also help you to squat until you get more proficient.

d You can also practise squatting against a wall, sliding your bottom down towards the floor.

Figure 16

If you can't sleep

If you do your exercises just before bedtime you may find they help you to sleep. Crazy though it may seem to anyone who is still

GETTING THE BALANCE RIGHT

in the early stages of pregnancy, where your eyes seem to snap shut at the slightest opportunity, sleep can be a problem later on. And there is nothing worse than lying in bed next to a gently snoring partner, worrying that if you don't get to sleep you will never make it through the next working day.

If you cannot get comfortable, try using extra pillows (see page 82). Some suggest that drinking camomile tea in the evenings will help you relax, but I found it tasted revolting! Probably the best advice, though the hardest to follow, is not to worry if you cannot sleep. Do something to take your mind off it. If you have a tolerant partner, switch on the bedside light and read for a bit. Get up and make yourself a drink. I used to be woken up in the latter stages by what appeared to be a football team practising inside me. Getting up and walking around for a while used to lull the baby for a while, so that I could doze off once I got back to bed.

Nasal congestion is another complaint in pregnancy, which may contribute to restlessness at night. If your nose is blocked up, you are more likely to breathe through your mouth and wake up feeling dry. Central heating makes things worse. You may not want to keep a window open in your bedroom during the winter months and lose all that precious warm air, but you should at least try to keep the atmosphere more humid by hanging humidifiers on the radiators or placing bowlfuls of water in the bedroom to evaporate.

You may also wake up during the night because you are too hot or too cold. You may need to change your normal bedcovers or nightwear. I found the duvet too hot and despite protests from my husband, insisted we went back to sheets and blankets for the duration. You will probably find cotton nightdresses or pyjamas more comfortable than those made of synthetic fabrics.

If you are restless because your skin is dry and itchy, remember to smother yourself in baby lotion before you go to bed and try a drop or two of baby oil in your bath.

If you are woken up with cramp in your leg, get your partner to grip your heel and push your foot up while he presses down on your knee with the other hand. If you don't want to wake him up, push your foot hard against the wall, stretching your ankle and pressing down on your own knee.

If you are being kept awake by low backache, get your partner to massage the area with his fingertips or the heel of his hand. A hot water bottle pressed to the small of your back can help too.

Checking for tension
If there seems to be no particular reason why you are awake, check your body for tension.
Hands: Clench your hands into fists, then relax. Stretch your fingers out as far as they will go. Then relax.
Legs: Squeeze your legs together and bend your feet up at the ankles. Then relax so that feet, knees and thighs roll outwards.
Shoulders: Hunch your shoulders hard, then relax. Pull your shoulders down as far as they will go. Relax.
Forehead: Frown hard, then relax. Raise your eyebrows as hard as possible and feel the tension in your forehead and scalp. Relax.
Jaws and lips: Grit your teeth and tighten your lips. Then relax your lips, mouth and jaw – don't forget your tongue. Let your jaw drop a little so that your lips are soft and slightly apart.

Check your breathing. You should be breathing slowly, gently and evenly. Pause after each breath out.

Solving problems
If you find you are lying awake because you are worrying about things to do with work, your pregnancy, or other problems, it may help to keep a notebook by the bed. Jot down the things that are bothering you and make a note of the ways in which you might deal with the situation. If you are worrying about the baby, for instance, write your particular worry down with a note to check with your doctor or ante-natal clinic.

Putting your problems down on paper and making a list of things to tackle in the morning or at the next possible opportunity can help you to clear your mind so that you get a good night's sleep.

Even if nothing seems to work, try not to get into a state about it. Make the most of the peace and quiet. After all, it will not be long before your night-time tranquillity is shattered by the demands of a small, hungry infant!

Some useful books about exercises are listed on page 183.

To find a teacher or an exercise class near you, get in touch with the West London Birth Centre (see page 185) enclosing a stamped, addressed envelope. They have details about other birth centres around the country. (Individual birth centres vary: some have their own teachers, film shows, talks, and libraries. Others are smaller, acting merely as information centres.)

You could also check the adult education centres for details of yoga classes. If the teacher is reluctant to accept pregnant women (some are) he or she may be able to refer to you to someone else in the area. Or you could contact the Iyengar Yoga Trust at 223A Randolph Avenue London W9. Tel: 01-624 3080.

6
Other people

Have I got enough time to dictate a couple of letters?

Working through pregnancy can be much easier if you have the support of those you work for and with. But although many women are now choosing to stay at work long beyond the time when their pregnancy is obvious, colleagues and employers are often ambivalent in their attitudes to pregnant workers.

This is partly because, despite their increasing numbers, working pregnant women are still very much in the minority amongst the female workforce. Things *are* changing – even television has given us a handful of programmes featuring a pregnant detective (Cagney and Lacey), a pregnant lawyer (Rumpole of the Bailey) and a pregnant launderette assistant (EastEnders).

Even so, if the term 'working woman' conjures up an image, it is certainly not one that includes a 'bump.' If you decide to work through your pregnancy you may well be the first woman at your particular place of employment to do so. As a result, your fellow workers and your employers might not know how to treat you: should they carry on as if everything was just the same as usual, should they handle you with kid gloves, or should they be even more eagle-eyed than ever to ensure your work is up to scratch?

When I was pregnant and working in Fleet Street I was lucky not to be a pioneer. Although my immediate boss (a woman) did not have children, I was not the first in my department to work through pregnancy. Those of my colleagues who had paved the way had already shown that being pregnant did not mean that your work had to suffer or that you had to become a passenger, thereby increasing the workload on others.

At the same time, because some of my colleagues knew just what it was like to be pregnant and hold down a fairly demanding job, they were the first to nag me about putting my feet up at lunchtime and, towards the end of the pregnancy, no one complained about my getting more than my fair share of working in the office, rather than being sent on out-of-town jobs.

If there was any additional pressure on me at all, it came from within myself. Because I knew, or knew of, women journalists at all levels who had worked well and effectively through their pregnancies, I felt I had to prove I was as determined and efficient as they had been.

Sorting out what you want from your colleagues

It is not always easy to sort out your own feelings and there may be a risk of refusing offers of help when you are pregnant just becuase you are trying to make the point that you can still do the job.

One teacher of twenty-eight worked until the thirty-second week of pregnancy. Her colleagues sometimes covered her playground duties or carried equipment for her. She said: 'I was reluctant to accept extra help, which caused extra work for others, simply, because of my condition. After all, I wasn't ill!'

A woman who worked in a greengrocer's shop said: 'I used to feel guilty asking people to lift something for me. You feel like a nuisance.'

A trainee clinical psychologist, aged twenty-six, who became pregnant during her final year of training, summed up the problem. 'Everyone told me to take it easy and let them know if it was difficult but on the other hand they were surprised if I turned up late for things. I felt very mixed up. I wanted to get my qualification on merit, so I didn't want special treatment, but on the other hand I did. I never really sorted this out.'

The attitudes of employers and workmates can vary enormously, from being over-protective to being downright difficult. In practice it seems to make no difference whether you work in a large organization or a small one: two different women doing exactly the same kind of job in similarly sized companies may have completely different experiences.

One twenty-six-year-old bank clerk said her bosses and colleagues went out of their way to make work easier for her. She worked for thirty-one weeks. She said: 'I was allowed to do a job which enabled me to sit down for a lot of the time.'

Problem areas
On the other hand, a bank clerk of twenty-seven, who stopped work as soon as she qualified for maternity pay at twenty-nine weeks, says: 'I did not expect an easy life but a little more consideration would have been welcome. Lifting and carrying was the most worrying aspect as I was involved with loading and unloading a cash dispenser. A girl was available to help quite often, but when she was not available I was expected to cope alone.

'Also, if a late finish was inevitable, no allowance was made for the fact that I was obviously tired after working eight hours. Lunch hours were a problem, too. There was a lot of pressure on me when I was busy. I was expected to cover many jobs without assistance. Unfortunately, many would believe a bank clerk's job is a sedentary one, but, on the contrary, it is a job which involves standing up continuously to answer enquiries from customers, attend to computer break-downs and so on.'

The women who took part in my pregnancy and work survey were fairly evenly divided into those who felt their bosses and colleagues *did* make work easier for them because they were pregnant and those who felt they did not. The most common form of help was simply offering to lift or carry heavy objects.

For some women – nurses in particular – this kind of help was invaluable, but, once again, varied from place to place and job to job.

A community nursing sister of thirty-five who worked for twenty-nine weeks says: 'Pregnant nurses are not given heavy patients for obvious reasons. Others took on my heavies.' She was more fortunate than the nurse of twenty-five who also worked for twenty-nine weeks but reported: 'My work involved lots of lifting of heavy patients and no help was given.'

Not enough staff to help
More often than not, however, it was not colleagues' unwillingness to help that was the problem, but the lack of enough staff to enable one woman to give another a hand.

A midwife of thirty-three, who worked night shifts because she had two older children, said: 'Much depended on the staffing levels – we were understaffed more often than not – and the workload.'

A nurse aged thirty-one, who also worked nights, said: 'When it was possible I was placed on wards where I wouldn't be lifting heavy patients all night. My colleagues helped as much as possible, but if there were only two members of staff on the ward, I had to do my share.'

Another nurse aged twenty-eight, said: 'I was told not to lift, but it is difficult if there is only you and one other nurse. Two nights before I was due to leave (at twenty-nine weeks) I had a 20-stone man in cardiac arrest. I coped at the time, but two days later I went into premature labour. They were able to stop the contractions but I had to spend six days on bed rest in the hospital, which was ironic as I had just stopped working there.'

Helpful colleagues
Women in other jobs found that colleagues were both willing and able to take on the heavy work and help in other ways. An assembly worker in an electronics factory, who was twenty-four and worked up to twenty-nine weeks, was allowed to sit down all day and said: 'People lifted heavy crates and boxes for me – although young men helped more than women.'

A manageress of a fashion shop, who was also twenty-four, said:

'My colleagues helped out more with heavy lifting and gave me more time to sit down when I needed.' A medical physics technician aged twenty-two said colleagues 'helped with heavy lifting work when asked', a receptionist of twenty-four said workmates 'carried things for me and generally tried to stop me rushing around', while a building society cashier aged twenty-six said that they 'wouldn't let me lift any heavy weights'.

Many women found their bosses sympathetic too. A conveyancer of twenty-six who worked until the thirty-seventh week said: 'A room with a bed was made available for me to have a nap at lunchtime and both my boss and my colleagues carried heavy files for me.' A private secretary aged thirty-seven who worked for thirty-five weeks said: 'There was less pressure on me to get things done and I was probably not asked to do some things which would otherwise have come my way.'

A nanny in a private home, who was twenty-three and worked for thirty-four weeks, said 'My employer said I could sleep when the baby was asleep and I did no housework of any kind.' A journalist aged twenty-five who worked up to a week before the birth said: 'I was given slightly less hectic and physical jobs to do and in the later weeks I spent most of my time in the office doing a lot of organizing and writing.'

A software engineer said she was allowed to work in the machine room which had air conditioning and was cooler than the office. A secretary with a sympathetic boss was allowed to spend the final month working mainly from home. A buyer for a large chain store was encouraged to spend more time in the office and less time travelling. A local government officer who suffered from oedema and high blood pressure was able to cut down her working hours so that she could get some bed rest in the afternoons.

Making your own suggestions

Obviously, if you have a good working relationship with your employer and colleagues, they are more likely to be considerate during your pregnancy. Even so, if they have no experience of pregnancy themselves, they may not realize that difficulties exist unless you tell them.

The way you tackle the situation is important. Bosses, by and large, do not like to be given ultimatums, nor do they relish having to handle any more problems than they already face in an average working day. It is a good idea to have a possible solution to suggest at the same time.

So you do not state flatly that you will not lift anything heavy. Instead you say you are worried about having to lift heavy things and would it be possible if X or Y gave you a hand. You do not announce that you cannot face the rush hour and will be leaving early. You explain that you are finding the journey difficult and wondered if you could halve your lunch hour so that you could leave at five instead of five-thirty. You may be surprised at the co-operation you get. As one clerical officer found: 'If I felt I couldn't physically cope with any job or had too much to do, I only had to ask and some other arrangements were made.'

Extra pressure at work
Despite helpful colleagues, however, some women find themselves under even more pressure during pregnancy, because they are not only expected to handle their routine work but also to train a successor or to complete certain projects before they go off on maternity leave. A specialist clerk in an American bank raised this point when she said: 'The concern of my colleagues was touching but there was actually more work to do – special projects were brought forward so that I could do them before I left.'

Sometimes the job itself allows little scope for flexibility. One woman, who worked as a fostering and adoption officer, explained: 'The job is physically and emotionally strenuous and there were days when I would liked to have worked shorter hours. The basic week is about thirty-seven and a half hours, but before I was pregnant I used to work between fifty and fifty-five. I cut back to about forty hours, but there was no decrease in the workload. It simply meant that more things piled up.'

Problems with company policy
Other women experienced difficulties, not with their immediate boss or with their colleagues or even with the workload, but with the personnel department or company policy.

An assistant editor was working for a firm which adopted Flexitime just when she became pregnant. In theory, this should have made life easier for her because, provided she worked during the core hours of 10 a.m. and 4 p.m., she could work the rest to suit herself. In practice, because she had to keep a lot of ante-natal appointments, it did not work out to her advantage at all.

The personnel department made it clear that she was entitled to have paid time off for ante-natal appointments, but only during core time. Any time taken off outside these hours, for whatever reason, was not counted as working time and therefore had to be made up. Since this woman's ante-natal clinic was near her home, not her place of work, this either meant that she had to travel in and out of town twice during the day in order to make sure the time off fell within core time, or she had to work later on some days to make up the lost time.

If her ante-natal appointment was at 9 a.m., for example, she had to make up for the hour she was not at work by working through a lunch hour or staying late at night. If she made the ante-natal appointment for 11 a.m., leaving the office at 10 a.m. to get there, she still had to return to work to clock up the time necessary after 4 p.m. to bring her hours worked that week up to the required total.

She says: 'Before Flexitime was introduced you were allowed to take any time off for ante-natal appointments between the hours of 9 a.m. and 5.15 p.m. So you could fix an appointment for first thing in the morning, then come in to work and finish at the usual time.

'Under the new system I ended up working until six nearly every evening and taking only twenty minutes lunch hour (illegally) just so that I was able to grab something in the canteen.

'Towards the end I was so exhausted that I simply had to leave at 5.15 each evening in the way that I would have been able to before Flexitime, and the firm went to some trouble to dock my final wages for the few hours in debit.

'And this was after I had been taking work home in order to leave everything in order and when I had never had so much as an hour off for the dentist in seven years there!'

A handful of women said that, far from being difficult about conceding any special arrangements, their bosses and colleagues were so concerned about their working through pregnancy that they were over-protective.

A woman of thirty-two, who worked as a care assistant in a

home for the elderly, said: 'I was rather killed with kindness. It was pleasant for a few weeks, then eventually I began to feel a bit useless and that I was being carried.'

If pregnancy holds back your career

Others found themselves with less to do, not because their bosses were trying to be helpful but because they felt that pregnancy had altered the woman's commitment to her career or that the image of a pregnant woman was not good for the company. A solicitor said: 'Towards the end they stopped sending me to court, partly out of consideration for me, but also I suspect because they did not feel it was good for the firm to have someone waddling in. You know what magistrates' courts are like!'

A secretary working in local government says she actually had difficulty getting re-graded during pregnancy. It was only when she returned to work after having the baby that the re-grading was confirmed.

A product manager who worked for thirty-five weeks said she felt very frustrated and exasperated at times. 'I am career-minded and did not want to be written off because of my pregnancy. But during the last month presentations were given to other people and various decisions were delayed until my successsor arrived, which was annoying. I also lost a promotion because I was pregnant.'

Another woman, with her feet firmly on the rungs of a career ladder in public relations, told me: 'I had made it quite plain that I would be coming back to work after having the baby, so no one doubted that work was still important to me. But once I had announced I was pregnant it was noticeable that no new accounts came my way. The company said it was just in case I found the workload too much, and they also felt it was better continuity if someone else, who wasn't going to be away for three months, took the work on.

'But since they weren't noted for their altruism I doubt very much whether they were really concerned for my welfare. And if they were just worried about their clients, what about those whose accounts I already handled?

'I suspect they were far more concerned about the company's image. They felt they might not hang on to new business if the clients concerned realized they were dealing with a pregnant woman. They thought that business lunches would be an embarrassment if I turned up looking like a balloon on legs.

'It's difficult to know how far those fears would have been justified. Certainly my existing clients were thrilled to hear of my pregnancy, never doubted my competance for one moment and took a touching interest in my progress. I had so many flowers sent to me in hospital that the post-natal ward looked like a florists' shop!'

Although this particular woman did not agree with the line the company had decided to take, she also felt there was no point in making an issue of it. She has since returned to work and is confident that it did her career no harm to go on 'hold' for a few months.

Other women are only too pleased by such paternalistic attitudes. As one, working for an international bank, pointed out: 'During pregnancy there are times when the last thing you want to do is to travel halfway round the world on business trips, gearing yourself up to talk to customers and so on, I don't have much time for the feminist attitudes that suggest there is something wrong if you are offered the chance of staying in the office and joining the research department instead. It's all a question of what is most practical.'

Sexual discrimination

It is almost impossible to gauge how far employers might be right in assuming that clients, customers or business contacts will baulk at having to deal with an obviously pregnant woman who also happens to be holding down a responsible job. Whether we like it or not, there are still people who find it hard to accept the concept of equality or the fact that a woman can be just as good in a job as a man.

Take the following true story, printed in *Working Woman* magazine. A man rang the offices of a direct-mail company based in Andover and asked to speak to their accountant. He was put through to a woman with whom he had the following conversation:

Him: 'Hello, may I speak to the company accountant?'
Her: 'Yes, that's me.'
Him: 'Could you please put me through to your boss.'

Her: 'I don't have one. I do the accounts.'
Him: 'You misunderstand me. I want to speak to the person in charge.'
Her: 'I don't misunderstand you, I am in charge of the accounts.'
Him: 'Could you please put me through to a man.'

If there are men who find it hard to take a woman seriously, then, presumably, the same type of men find it impossible to cope with a pregnant woman at all on a business level.

Some women felt that the covert sexual discrimination which existed in their companies surfaced when they were pregnant. A civil engineer who worked until the twenty-nine weeks said: 'There was so much discrimination in the job anyway that I decided not to be frail and feminine. As a result I think I overdid it a bit.

'But I had always been determined not to refuse to do anything – like climbing high ladders on sites even though I hate heights – in case they said it was because I was a woman. And that was still the way I felt in pregnancy. In fact, nobody knew I was pregnant until the fifth month. I didn't tell anybody.'

The departmental head of a market research company said: 'Although they always denied it, there was a lot of resistance to the idea of women getting into top positions. And there was also a feeling that the whole idea of women working through pregnancy and then taking maternity leave was all very well, but when you are running a company you really can't afford to have people taking time off to do silly things like having babies.'

Inevitably, the women who encountered these kinds of attitudes found they had two courses open to them – to grin and bear it or to wash their hands of that particular company altogether. Those in the latter category decided that when they returned to work it would be for a different firm. Some, like the market researcher, went freelance.

Others, like one public relations consultant, decided that the best course was to treat it as a minor irritant. 'At six months my boss gently suggested that I might not be up to meeting new clients. And it was difficult trying to talk business with a six-month growth in front of you. With some people it does reduce your credibility. I had to accept that that could be the attitude of clients so I stayed in the background for a while. I had a wonderful telephone manner, but when people met me their jaw dropped. You just have to overcome it, prove yourself. And if you do win their respect you can do very well out of it.'

Even in jobs where women are treated as equals and where good provision has been made for maternity leave and pay, there may be undercurrents of feeling. One union press officer said: 'I'm lucky that the organization I work for has gone beyond the current legislation concerning paid maternity leave and that their attitude to pregnant women therefore tends to be better than some. Pregnancy is not seen as a major crime.

'But at the same time, although you are allowed generous time off to keep ante-natal appointments and so on, there is a general feeling that they are somehow doing you a big favour and that you should be grateful. I think it's wrong that women should be made to feel almost apologetic for being fertile.'

Problems with maternity leave
In companies where the management views maternity rights with some disfavour, or even where an individual boss disagrees with company policy, women face more specific problems.

A woman working for a large publishing company found herself under tremendous pressure when her department head discovered she intended to take all the leave to which she was entitled. She said: 'Although the company employed a lot of women and they had dealt with a lot of pregnancies, it was his first experience of the situation and he had no concept of what was involved. I don't think he even realized there was a statutory allowance of leave.

'After the initial congratulations when I announced my pregnancy, the subject of how much leave I would be taking cropped up. I think he assumed I would be having about three months altogether. When I told him I was going to take the full eleven weeks before and twenty-nine weeks afterwards, he was appalled. He seemed to feel that I was getting one over on him, that it was a holiday. Throughout the rest of my pregnancy he was really horrible to me.

'I know I'm good at my job and that it would be difficult to replace me so it was rather flattering in a way. But he kept on saying that I was letting down my workmates, that they would have to carry the load and it was a miserable time. I had arranged to have the baby at home, but instead of getting congratulations from him when the baby was born, I got another vitriolic letter. At this stage he was trying to make me come back to a different work pattern, working different hours, although when I had taken the job originally it had been agreed that I would do fewer hours than others in the department, because I already had a child and other commitments. The only thing that kept me going was knowing that I was in the right.

'He didn't get his way and when I went back to work, on the original terms, things were still pretty bad. It took about a year and a half for things to get back to normal, yet even today he made a joke about my never getting pregnant again.'

If you have no statutory rights
Unfortunately many women find themselves pregnant before they have worked for a particular firm long enough to qualify for any statutory rights to return to work after the birth of the baby. This can also affect the conditions of work and their feelings about work during pregnancy.

One accountant said: 'I had worked for this particular firm for less than two years, so I knew that they did not have to hold my job open for me. But I made it quite clear that I wanted to come back and I asked if I could take some unpaid maternity leave.

'The whole thing dragged on for several months and I found it had a real impact on the work I was supposed to be doing. I was worrying about the future all the time and it also seemed hard to put as much effort into everything if I wasn't, after all, going to come back to my desk in a few months' time. In the end they did agree to my suggestions, but by that time I was feeling pretty fed-up with them all. From their general attitudes towards me, and mothers in general, I got the distinct impression that in career terms I'd be better off elsewhere. So I left anyway and found myself another job with a different, more enlightened, company when the baby was six months old.'

Another woman who found herself in a similar situation decided to ask for maternity leave 'as I enjoyed my job and intended to return after the baby was born'.

She says: 'At first my boss was very evasive. He did not discuss the situation with me openly and, in fact, made arrangements to employ someone else in my post. This was, of course, put to me as "the needs of the company" which could not cope with my having a few months off.

'I was very upset indeed, not only at losing my job but also at the way it had been handled. I think the least that my boss could have done was to talk openly to me about what he was going to do. I made my feelings known to other people in the company, but no one was prepared to take my boss on about it.

'Because of this situation I decided to screw as much money as I could out of the company at least cost to myself. I therefore announced that I would be working mainly from home and thus I was able to work until just two weeks before my daughter arrived. It also meant that I did not have to travel in the rush hour.

'Owing to a certain amount of guilt felt by both my boss and other people in the company, who felt to some degree that I had had a raw deal, I managed to get away with quite a lot!

'Now that my daughter has arrived I still feel very upset about what happened at work. I did enjoy my work a lot and put in a lot of overtime and energy in building up a good research team.

'I feel I have had the rough end of a lot of prejudice which existed in the company towards women. Two women in the company had taken pregnancy leave and by the way the directors talked about this you could see they considered it to be a very difficult thing to cope with and to be avoided if at all possible.'

If you are not the first woman in your workplace to work through pregnancy, you may, fairly or unfairly, find that other people's attitudes to you are coloured by the way your predecessors behaved. Although this can be a disadvantage if their pregnancies caused real difficulties, it can be a positive advantage if everything went smoothly and bosses and colleagues know from experience that having a pregnant woman on the team is not a liability.

As one doctor pointed out: 'Everyone was pretty good about everything, even though I'd planned to work longer than I eventually did. (I had to stop towards the end and rest as the baby wasn't growing enough.) The other woman I was working with had worked through two pregnancies, so they'd been through it all before. They were used to women doctors going off to have babies.'

A chain-store buyer added: 'The boss I worked for when I joined the company had had two children while she'd been there, so everyone knew – including me – that it could be done.'

Practical and emotional support

It seems clear that pregnant women need not just practical help, but emotional support too. While they have no wish to be cocooned or treated like pieces of very fragile china, neither do they want to be made to feel a nuisance or a freak. They simply want people to accept their decision to work on, and to give them the same kind of respect as before, while offering them the consideration you might afford anyone who has certain physical limitations.

As one woman said: 'Of course it was nice when people offered to carry things for me – but it was annoying when some tried to make decisions for me. Pregnancy doesn't affect the brain.'

It is partly this fear of being treated differently that makes some women decide to postpone the announcement of their pregnancy to their workmates for as long as possible. As several put it: 'I didn't want to be fussed over.'

The union press officer added: 'Once it's obvious that you are pregnant you get sick of the same old questions from well-meaning people. Towards the end, I felt like hanging a placard round my neck saying when the baby was due, when I was giving up work and so on. Having a baby is a big thing, but it isn't the total commitment of your life and it's very irritating when your mind is on something else to have to explain everything to everyone all the time.'

A pub manageress who worked right up until the last moment echoed this view: 'The concern by customers was hard to take, being repeatedly asked the same old questions.'

Being asked questions is one thing – being given well-meaning if misplaced advice is another. A shop assistant said: 'It was difficult sometimes when customers told me worrying things, like "you shouldn't stretch up or you'll get the cord round the babies head". Even though you know it's nonsense, it gets to you.'

Many women, however, reported that they enjoyed the extra attention that pregnancy brought them. 'It really made me feel special,' said one clerical worker. 'People in the office were interested and caring, and I loved every minute.'

Improved working relationships
Another positive aspect reported by some women was that their pregnancy improved relationships at work by providing an area of common ground.

A sub-editor on a newspaper, whose job involved working with printers in an otherwise exclusively male environment, said that the men became rather more protective towards her and therefore more helpful than usual. They would nag her about not drinking and tell her not to rush about so much. 'Many of them had young children or grandchildren of their own; they were genuinely interested in my pregnancy.'

A woman working in public relations took on a new client when she was eight months pregnant. 'Two of his daughters were expecting babies at the same time as me so we had something in common. We got on very well – it strengthened our relationship.'

And a secretary who had found her new boss rather cold and impersonal, discovered that he had a human side. She says: 'It was a difficult situation at first because he was brought in to do the job when my original boss was moved sideways in the company. I had been working for him for four years and we got on very well, but I wasn't able to move with him. Although my new boss never said anything, I think he would rather have appointed his own secretary than take me over, so to speak.

'Then, when I told him I was pregnant and we discussed leaving dates, it turned out that his wife was expecting a baby too. And from then on we got on much better on every level. In fact, although I hadn't originally decided whether or not to return to work, I did in the end take maternity leave.'

Social life after work
On the other hand, some women find that they begin to drift away from colleagues when they are pregnant. In some jobs for example, the social life after work is almost as important as what goes on nine-to-five, so pregnancy may make a difference.

A television director said: 'Going for a drink after the programme, winding down, talking about what went wrong, what went right, was always part of the job. But things started to change when I was pregnant. By the end of the afternoon my ankles were starting to swell up, I felt exhausted and all I wanted to do was to get home and put my feet up. You do start to lose contact a bit.

'In a way, it's a good thing. While you are pregnant you start to develop a whole new perspective on life. However important work is, from now on it is only going to be part of your life. You have to begin to distance yourself a bit, because you are going to have other responsibilities.'

A news reporter said: 'I always liked going for a drink with the rest of the "lads" after work but when I got pregnant there seemed little point. I couldn't drink, I didn't want to stand around in smoky pubs, and although I missed the chat and the gossip, all I really wanted to do was go home. Looking back, it seems to me that pregnancy marks a change in all kinds of relationships. Whereas before I'd been drawn to people who had the same kind of life-style, in and out of work, now I felt I had more in common with people who had children, who knew what it was all about. And they were the ones who didn't hang around in pubs but went straight home.'

Greater popularity at work

By and large, though, many women felt their pregnancy somehow made them more popular particularly among male colleagues. One office worker said: 'I was amazed at how friendly everyone was. People I hardly knew congratulated me. Lots of the men told me how great I was looking. In fact, I was paid a lot more attention than normal.'

If you are not prepared for this it can come as a bit of a surprise, particularly when even those who are not close friends seem to have no hesitation in giving the bump a friendly pat or asking if they can feel the baby moving. The solicitor said she was rather taken aback when one of the partners, who was normally aloof, started coming up to her and giving her stomach a pat.

It is hard to pinpoint why this kind of thing should happen. It may be something to do with pheromones – the subliminal scents given off by the body that, in the animal world, at least, have been proved to play a powerful role in attracting male to female. It may be something to do with body language. A woman who is happy to be pregnant, who sends out positive signals about herself and her body, is quite likely to get a positive reponse back.

It may even be that from a man's point of view a pregnant woman is obviously a sexual being, but one who poses no particular sexual threat. As one psychologist put it: 'Around a pregnant women men don't feel they have to straighten their ties and push out their chests. They can relax, and even flirt without fear of the consequences.'

You may feel that people are taking liberties, with this kind of behaviour, however, and you could be right. Psychologist Jane Firbank points out that the amount of physical contact that exists between people has as much to do with status as it does with sex.

'We always feel more able to touch people lower in status than ourselves. The boss can pat a junior manager on the back and say "well done old man", but the reverse situation would be impossible. We all feel free to touch children or animals. And the fact that women have lower status than men in society can be illustrated by the fact that they are given less personal space than men by strangers.

'If you watch a male shop assistant moving through a crowded store he will physically touch a woman customer on the arm to get her to move out of the way. He is more likely to speak to a male customer.

'And not only do women have a low status in society generally, pregnancy itself has pretty low status. Look at all the studies which indicate how hospital staff treat pregnant women like idiots. No one gets extra Brownie points for being a mother or even an expectant one.

'It may also be that in a work situation the very fact of pregnancy signals that a woman now has another set of priorities which may remove her from the whole scenario of office politics and any power or influence she had.'

Personally, I find that a fairly depressing explanation and would prefer instead to think that even today the most hard-bitten of us still have a wonder and admiration for the miracle of birth.

It is that emotional response that breaks down the barriers, that fascination which prompts people to pat or touch, to ask to feel new life move.

Keeping a professional attitude

There is no doubt that the attitudes of other people at work, from the managing director to the tea-boy, can make a big difference to the ease with which you cope in pregnancy and the enjoyment you can continue to get from your work as the months progress. But your attitude is important too.

Being late because you have suffered from a bad spell of morning sickness is one thing. Being later because you stopped off at Mothercare to choose cot covers is another.

Marking time until you can collect your maternity pay does no one any favours, least of all any women who may follow in your footsteps. Working all hours just to prove some kind of point and ending up confined to bed with high blood pressure is almost as bad.

A television producer, who was one of a team working on a pilot show when she discovered she was pregnant, felt obliged to carry on long after she wanted to stop work. 'The programme was partly my idea, so I felt I couldn't renege on it. Also, I was working with terribly high-powered people so I felt I had to pull my weight. There was a really competitive feeling. But at thirty-two weeks the midwife told me my blood pressure was really high and she forbade me to go to work. I had to stay in bed.

'I had to ring the office and let them down at a critical period. Although they were able to find someone to replace me I felt terribly guilty.'

It is not always easy to step back from a situation and take a long-term view, but if you are planning to work through pregnancy it is essential to do that if you can. That may mean being more realistic and less optimistic about the workload you will be able to cope with. On the other hand, no one will thank you if you use your pregnancy as an excuse for shirking work. Either way, it is worth remembering that you are more likely to get the kind of consideration you might need from your colleagues if you also consider them.

Many women find the interest and concern displayed by their colleagues and employers both flattering and helpful; a positive contribution to a working pregnancy. But if you are faced with attitudes that are less than helpful, try not to let the situation get you down. Bring specific issues out into the open if you can, because others may not realize what is bothering you, but try not to waste too much time and energy fretting about what cannot be changed. Worrying will not help you or the baby.

In career terms, you may find yourself marking time during pregnancy. The reactions of others to you in these months may make you think again about the wisdom of staying with a particular firm, but don't make any hasty decisions. After all, the time you spend working in pregnancy is short compared with the rest of your working life.

7

At home

Getting the support of workmates and employers can be a great help to the pregnant working woman: getting the support of a partner at home can be even more crucial.

All the studies show that, despite all the lip-service towards equality, the woman does more work in the home, even when both the man and the woman work full-time. The Social Trends report issued in 1986 revealed that men working full-time had 33.5 free hours a week, compared with their female counterparts who had only 24.6 free hours.

One research survey carried out in London found that men with full-time jobs spent ten hours a week on household tasks, and women with full-time jobs spent twenty-three hours.

Even though many men claim (and many wives support their claims) to share the housework, independent observers who clocked up the chores the men actually did, found that the time they put in dusting, cooking or whatever, was not nearly so great as either they or their wives had thought.

It would seem, then, that quite a lot of the work women do at home is taken for granted, both by men and by the women themselves. A University of California researcher discovered, when studying a large number of families where the wives worked, that the husbands *did* do more housework and child care than in households where the wives did not work, but the amount of time spent on these chores did not approach equality. Nevertheless, these husbands and wives frequently believed that they shared the work equally.

What help will you need?

So, whether you are happy with your current arrangements for running the home and dealing with the chores or not, now is a good time to sit down and re-evaluate the situation. Pregnancy does make extra demands on the body and if you are working as well you will need help at home.

Countries like Holland and Finland, where pregnant women and new mothers can get home helps, have low perinatal mortality rates. Some experts have suggested that there is a link between these two facts.

For most women in this country, the most likely source of such help is going to be a husband. And, to be fair to husbands, most of them appear to rise to the occasion.

Two-thirds of the women who took part in my survey said that their husbands helped more during pregnancy. And some of those who said their husbands did not help more, pointed out that this was because they had always done their share anyway.

The extent to which the husbands helped varied. One just took over the vacuuming, because his wife had been advised at the ante-natal class not to do it. A lot took over the cooking at night (particularly if the wife suffered from nausea); others took over the more strenuous jobs like mowing the lawn or washing the windows, making the beds or doing the monthly bulk shopping. Most gave a hand with housework, a few took on the ironing.

Only a few wives said they were 'spoiled rotten', getting tea in bed in the mornings or having their breakfast cooked for them.

In many cases, however, the household arrangements seemed to be somewhat ad hoc, with the husband taking over particular chores only when the wife made it clear she could not face them. It might be a better idea to sit down with your partner at an early stage of the pregnancy, or even when you are still in the planning stages, to work out how you would prefer to share the load at home.

Talk it over
Talking about the way you feel and the help you think you might need is important. At the beginning of a pregnancy your body is undergoing momentous changes. You may feel sick, and incredibly tired. At the same time your mood may swing wildly from elation to depression, and the most trivial incident may trigger tears. Yet outwardly you look much the same as usual and unless you can explain to your partner just what is going on, you are unlikely to get either the support or the sympathy you need at home.

A receptionist aged twenty-four, who worked until the twenty-ninth week of pregnancy in order to be able to claim all her maternity pay, says: 'Work was very tiring and my husband used to lose patience with me. I was always fit and not a lazy person, but in the early weeks of pregnancy I was tired all the time. I couldn't be bothered to cook or to work with him in the garden or do the general things we always did. He found that very hard to accept. We had spent seven years on our own and we are very close. I think he resented the fact that I was having a baby because it was coming between us.

'I found working full-time and all of this just too much to cope with and I wouldn't like to have to go through it again. I don't think for a moment I am alone in this situation.'

Happily for this woman, things did get better. She said that once her pregnancy began to show, her husband became more considerate and no longer objected to taking over some of the jobs she had previously done. And once she left work 'life between us got back to normal.'

It does seem a shame, though, that the early months had proved so tense. Yet the whole question of who does what in the home tends to be emotionally charged, whether the subject raises its head during pregnancy or not.

Why men do not co-operate

Marjorie Shaevitz, who has written a book called the *Superwoman Syndrome* (Fontana, 1985) says: 'Frankly I know of no area in our lives – including sex, children, money or in-laws – concerning which there is more polarization between the sexes. I don't know of another area in which male and female ways of thinking, feeling and action could be more different.'

She suggests there are a number of different reasons why men do not do their share of housework, even when their wives work. Partly it is tradition, partly it is self-interest and partly it is ignorance. She says: 'Some men have no idea of what is involved in keeping a household running smoothly and how that relates to their quality of life. They are totally unaware of the organization, activities and enormity of the work and the skills it requires.'

She adds: 'Many men put everything they have into their work because they feel financially responsible. Even when their wives work, men feel that ultimately it is up to them to provide. As a consequence, they spend all their time (mentally and physically) preparing for work. Almost everything else seems irrelevant.' But she also suggests that women may sometimes have themselves to blame.

'One of the major barriers to getting help with housework is that women do not ask for it. Men don't feel responsible for housework, so they don't think about it unless someone brings it to their attention.'

Pregnancy is a good time to bring it to their attention. The results of my survey suggest that, in general, men are more willing than usual to share the load at this time. Strike while the iron is hot! If you are working as well as growing a baby you will need time to rest, and the only way you will get that time is by cutting down on some of the household chores, or by getting someone else to do them.

Organizing the chores

Whether you are planning to do either or both, organization is the key. The trouble with housework is that it just seems to creep up on you. Because it is so much a part and parcel of everyday life, it is hard to step back and take a good look at it as a whole. But I think it is worth trying to do this, to tackle the problem as if it was a job you were going to be paid to do. Instead of treating housework as the things you do in the role of housewife, think of it as your responsibility as a house manager.

As a manager it is your job to work out what tasks have to be done, how best to do them, and who should do them. Sit down and work out a list encompassing all the household chores and the frequency with which they need to be done.

Now go back through the list and check off each item by asking yourself the question 'Is this really necessary?' If the answer is 'no', cross it off. Then go back through the list again to see if some of the daily jobs could be done every other day, the weekly jobs every other week and so on.

After all, if you have enough cutlery and crockery, does it really matter if the washing up is not done after every meal, but stacks up for a while? There are some things you probably won't be able to cut down very much for the sake of hygiene – washing the kitchen floor or cleaning the loo, for instance – but in other cases it will not do any harm if you drop your standards a little.

Now think about the way you normally do some of the chores and ask yourself if you can adapt your usual system to make it less tiring. When I was pregnant I used to do the ironing sitting down. It took slightly longer, but it did not wear me out so much. In principle it is a good idea to sit rather than stand whenever you can. You can peel the potatoes just as easily sitting at the kitchen table with a bowl of water as you can standing at the sink. Better still, plump for baked potatoes which only need a quick scrub.

Improving on your equipment
Take a look at the equipment in your house and ask yourself whether you can afford to improve some of your resources. It may sound daft, but even buying a decent potato peeler or a couple of sharp kitchen knives can speed up certain tasks and the less time spent on the chores the better.

If you have an efficient vacuum cleaner with a couple of useful attachments you will not have to get on your hands and knees with a dustpan and brush quite so much. Even lengthening the flex means you will not waste time and energy plugging and unplugging as you move from room to room.

If you can afford it, it is worth considering some of the larger and more expensive household appliances. If you don't have a freezer, or if yours is quite small, it might be worth getting a larger one, Not only will you be able to cut down on the number of shopping trips necessary by stocking up once a month with things like bread, meat, fish and frozen vegetables but you can minimize the cooking, either by keeping a supply of frozen convenience foods or, better still, by making sure that each time you do cook you make enough for several extra meals which can then be frozen.

Making cooking easier
If you are working through pregnancy, often the last thing you feel like doing when you come home is cooking the evening meal. So if you have an oven with a timer make the most of it. You might not want to leave meat or fish sitting around all day, particularly in the summer, but there are tasty and nutritional alternatives. How about vegetable casseroles, baked potatoes that can be topped with cheese, ratatouille, gratin dauphinois, macaroni cheese, or cauliflower cheese?

An alternative to using an oven timer is to buy a slow electric hot-pot. This will cope with a variety of different meals, from whole joints to casseroles, soups to stuffed marrow. Of course, whether you use an oven with a timer or a slow cook-pot, someone still has to prepare the meal, but you may find you have more energy in the mornings than in the evenings.

You might prefer to invest in a pressure cooker. Although many people still tend to be rather frightened of pressure cookers, the modern ones have built-in safety devices and, according to a friend of mine who has worked through two pregnancies and also happens to be a home economist, they are the most time-saving domestic devices apart from micro-wave ovens.

You can use pressure cookers for anything from cakes to casseroles, and since they come with trivets and vegetable baskets it is possible to cook a two-course meal in three-quarters of the time it would normally take, or even less.

Microwaves, according to the home economist, are even better. She says: 'They reheat things from frozen very well and in a fraction of the usual time. An uncooked joint of beef weighing about 3 pounds takes eighteen minutes. Vegetables stay crunchy, which means you get the roughage you need in pregnancy and another big bonus is that you can cook individual portions on most ordinary kitchen crockery and even some plastics, which saves on the washing up.

'Even when it comes to cooking things which won't save you time – like pasta, for instance – the advantage is that you don't have to worry about keeping an eye on the food in case it boils over. You can sit down and put your feet up while you wait.'

Dishwashers and tumble driers

I have always felt that a dishwasher was more of a luxury than a necessity, although people who have them tend to claim that they cannot imagine how they ever managed without them. And it does seem true that men who would not otherwise sully their hands with washing-up liquid, seem to have no objections to loading and operating a dishwasher.

A tumble drier, on the other hand, is worth its weight in gold. Apart from the fact that you no longer have depressing lines of soggy clothes hanging around the house on wet days, and you save time by not having to hang clothes out, it does cut down the amount of ironing necessary. And. of course, you are only planning to iron things that actually show, aren't you?

Counting the cost

If money is tight, the idea of being able to go out and buy any major of household equipment may seem out of the question. But remember that all of these things will prove their worth after the baby is born. So before you dismiss the idea altogether, think about your budget as a whole. What you are planning to spend on baby equipment? Is it really necessary?

My first child slept in a borrowed cot, was taken out first in a borrowed baby sling, later a borrowed carry cot, later still in a borrowed buggy. I borrowed a high chair and a baby walker. I bought a second-hand baby bath and car seat. At current prices these items, new, would cost more than £250. Yet you can get a tumble drier for around £120, a microwave for around £220, a freezer for around £150.

It is only natural to want the best for your baby, but if you are a hard-working mum-to-be, then the best may have more to do with how you look after yourself, and the amount of rest you can get, rather than having a nursery full of spanking new things.

Shopping for food

The trouble with running a house is that it is rather like being on a treadmill, and even if you manage to slow down a little you cannot stop altogether. Some things still have to be done. The house may not get spring-cleaned but unless you want to live in a pig-sty you will at least have to give the place the occasional 'lick and a promise'. Even if you opt for salads and lots of fresh fruit as the bulk of your meals, there will still be some food preparation to be done. And the kitchen cupboards will not replenish their stocks by themselves.

Cut down the amount of time that actually has to be spent at the shops by getting into the habit of making lists. Some items will always be needed – bread, perhaps, or cereals. Keep the basic list pinned somewhere handy, such as in the kitchen, and whenever something is running low, add that item to this list before you put the old packet back in the cupboard. If you use the last of anything, add it to the list straight away. Once you have restocked, cross it off.

It is also a good idea to find out if any of your local shops will deliver food and if you can order by phone. If you are going to spend a reasonable amount they might be willing to do this. My greengrocer, for example, used to deliver orders of over £5 free of charge. Make the most of your milkman, too. He may not only deliver milk and other dairy items like cheese, butter and yoghurt, but also bread, eggs, potatoes and fruit juice.

If you live in certain parts of London and you suscribe to Prestel you can use your television and their Telecard Supershop service to order from a range of over 3500 brand-name supermarket items, including a selection of fresh meat and vegetables, from the comfort of your own home.

Prices compare with good-quality London supermarkets and work out cheaper than most late-night convenience stores. You pay by cheque on delivery, which is free providing your bill comes to more than £35. The minimum order is £15, delivery charge £2.

At the time of writing, it costs £6.50 a quarter to subscribe to Prestel and you also need to buy a special keypad to call up and send information. When Telecard Supershop was launched this cost £99.95. To make your order, you call up the lists of products on the screen or use the Product and User Guide supplied. When you have selected an item you tap in the code number and enter the quantity required. To help you keep a check on how much you are spending, a running total is shown after you order each product.

The service was initially launched to cover the boroughs of Hammersmith, Fulham, Westminster, Kensington and Chelsea, Camden, and Wandsworth but plans were underway to extend the service to a further nine boroughs.

In the not so distant future this kind of shopping by television will probably be available to most of us who can afford it. But for those of us who have no choice but to slog round supermarkets, remember that late-night shopping is not usually so crowded as Saturday shopping. Find out which of your local supermarkets stay open on Thursday and Friday nights, and which ones employ staff to help with packing and loading.

If you have not got a car, do at least get a shopping basket with wheels.

Shopping for the baby

Shopping for food is one thing: shopping for the new baby is another. Once again, you need to draw up a list. My advice is to get as little as possible to begin with. Once you get the baby home you will soon work out what else you need and that way you will not find yourself with lots of bits and pieces that you never use. Also, many women feel it is tempting fate to buy too much too early on. Many shops will allow you to buy equipment, but will hold it for delivery until after the baby is born. If anything does go wrong, you can get a refund without having to go through the difficult process of taking things back.

You may decide to do the shopping bit by bit or wait until you have finished work and shop in one or two major expeditions when you have more time. Whichever method you choose it is probably worth adding certain items to your household shopping list each week. There is not a lot of fun in choosing cotton wool or baby lotion, so those kind of things might as well be bought along with the groceries. And you could also consider the advantages of armchair shopping. For example, Mothercare have a mail order service, or you can order by phone (see page 71). You could get everything you needed this way, from nappy pins to baby alarms and if anything turns out not to be suitable, you can get a refund or exchange it provided you return it within two weeks.

Sharing the chores

Once you have drawn up some kind of masterplan in your role as household manager, decided which chores are essential and which are not, worked out labour-saving ways of doing some things and strategies for tackling others, your next task is to decide on the division of labour.

At this point, if not before, it is time to show the list to your husband and discuss it with him. Without sounding like a nag or a martyr, explain how much work is involved, suggest areas in which you would most like help and ask for his ideas on tackling the situation. As I said earlier, most husbands seem willing to do more than usual when their wives are pregnant, but don't get mad if the immediate response is not as helpful as you had hoped. Ask nicely, don't demand. What you want is a willing volunteer, not a reluctant conscript.

Getting paid help

Another thing you should consider is the possibility of paying someone outside the home to do some of the chores for you. It need not cost a fortune – employing someone for just a couple of hours a week to do the ironing and the more difficult cleaning jobs might be well worth the expense. An offices service supervisor did this, and was pleased with the results. She says: 'I'd worked full-time and run the home for nine years, but during my pregnancy, when my husband realized how tired I was, he suggested we got a cleaning lady to come in for four hours a week. She was an absolute godsend and a real tonic.'

Many women are curiously reluctant to spend money on outside help for the home, even when they can afford it. Marjorie Shaevitz suggests that this attitude partly reflects the conflicts women have about giving to themselves.

Paying someone to do something rather than doing it yourself is somehow seen as an unnecessary indulgence. Or it may be that women who work because they choose to rather than because they need the money, do not want their husbands to feel they are neglecting them *because* they work.

If you dismiss the idea of hiring help, ask yourself why? Are you sure you could not cut down on any other items of expenditure to cover the cost? Are you sure you are not struggling on unaided through a misplaced sense of guilt, a feeling that a woman should do her own housework? Or because, deep down, you are trying to win an extra round of applause? Or because you think you should be some kind of superwoman?

Why is it all right to pay someone to fix the iron if your husband can't, but not to pay someone to do the ironing if *you* can't? And which is more important, getting the rest you and your baby need, or personally getting the creases out of your husband's shirts?

You don't have to go the whole hog and employ a daily. Work out how much help you need and then find someone to fit the bill. The cheapest way is to put a card in the window of your local newsagent's. Someone coming for one morning a month might be enough, or perhaps you know a teenager who would like to earn some extra cash for the odd hour here or there.

Your relationship with your partner

The whole question of who does what in the home is often a thorny one for working couples, as I have said. But when you are pregnant the whole relationship may undergo all kinds of changes. To begin with, it is not always easy for a man to appreciate the differences pregnancy can make, particularly in the early months. If you have been used to sharing a fairly active social life, he may find it hard to come to terms with the fact that his night owl now tends to fall asleep in the early evening and the last thing she wants to do is to go out for a meal, see a film or entertain friends. He may have accepted the fact that a baby would change his life, but he may not have expected the changes to come so quickly.

At the same time, you may be feeling far from emotionally stable yourself. However much you may have wished for the pregnancy, now that you know you are pregnant your feelings may be mixed. You may feel elated and yet trapped. You may have doubts about becoming a mother, about labour, about whether the baby will be all right. You may be worrying about work, about how you will cope, about whether or not you want to go back to work afterwards. All in all, this is a time when you want some reassurance and support, yet your partner's attitude may merely be resentful.

Even before you lose your waistline or feel those first fluttering movements, the baby will probably be very real to you. But to your man, the changed you, not the baby is the reality. And even if he is proud at the prospect of becoming a father, he may also feel trapped by a new sense of responsibility. Even though you are working, even though you may be intending to return to work after the baby is born, he is probably only too well aware that if anything happens to alter those plans, the total financial burden will be his.

Arguments about work
It can also be a problem if you discover that the scenario you have been planning is different from the one he had in mind. A journalist told me: 'I'd always assumed that I would work for as long as possible, take some maternity leave and go back to work when the baby was about six months old. But when I said something about it to my husband I realized that he had different ideas. He wanted me to stop work at about twenty-eight weeks and he thought I shouldn't make any plans about returning until the baby was much older. He didn't understand how important my job was to me, or how I could possibly think about what *I* wanted as well as what would be best for the baby. In the end I got my way and he now admits that it has all worked out well. But there were some pretty heated discussions at a time when I really wanted my confidence boosted not undermined.'

The reverse situation can also occur. An accountant said: 'When I found out I was pregnant I was really happy and immediately started to make plans about leaving work and starting to decorate the nursery and so on, But my husband said there was no reason for me not to carry on – in fact, he thought we should both go on earning as long as possible. It annoyed me, as I didn't feel we desperately needed the money and I didn't much like the job I was in anyway. In fact, I stopped as soon as I qualified for maternity pay, which he couldn't really argue about.'

Sheila Kitzinger says, in her book *Pregnancy and Childbirth*, 'Pregnancy is not merely a waiting time. It is a time for working out together what you value in your relationship and what kind of world you both want to create for your child. This is not a question of making a nursery and buying things ready for your baby, but of helping each other to change from people who are responsible just for themselves into a mother and father, with the new responsibility that parenthood brings.'

In an ideal world, of course, we would all sit down at the start of a relationship, or at least when it was clear that the relationship was going to lead to marriage or something similarly committed, and discuss our hopes and expectations. In practice, a lot of our feelings stay undefined and undiscussed, surfacing to cause friction only when something else, such as pregnancy, makes us pay attention to more than the here-and-now. But there is no point in trying to bottle up emotions until they boil over. The sooner you can talk things out, the better.

Your sex-life during pregnancy

Pregnancy can be a very loving time, when the joy you share about the forthcoming baby can bring you closer together. But it can also be a time when the relationship seems strained to the utmost, far from the romantic interlude you may have hoped for. And if pregnancy is affecting your sexual response to each other as well, then things may become very tense indeed.

Pregnancy need not mean the end of a satisfying love life. Many couples make love right through pregnancy and many women find their sex drive is much stronger. On the other hand, if you are very tired you will only want to *sleep* in bed. If you suffer from nausea or sickness, love-making may be the last thing you want to do. And in the later stages you may just feel too large and uncomfortable to be indulging in anything athletic.

Some men, too, find it difficult to accept the physical changes in their woman (although I have never heard of one who objected to the sudden appearance of a cleavage).

Others worry about hurting the baby or, subconsciously, of hurting their penis. Neither will happen, of course, but there are some love-making positions which you may find more comfortable than others. It is worth experimenting. Try sitting on the bed with your man kneeling in front of you, or lie like spoons so that he enters from the back.

Sort out any problems
If your sex-life does suffer more than a temporary set-back, don't ignore the situation and hope everything will sort itself out. Do try to discuss it. The dangers of not doing so can be considerable, both at home and at work.

To begin with, recent studies have shown that how well you do at work can be affected by problems at home, in just the same way that hassles at work can upset the domestic status quo. There is also the possibility that, lacking the emotional closeness you need at home, you will turn to male colleagues at work, particularly if they have already been showing you extra attention since your pregnancy.

This is not as fanciful as it might seem. I personally know two working women who had affairs while they were pregnant. Not surprisingly, both marriages ended in divorce.

One of these women, a social worker, explained what happened. 'Looking back, I think our marriage was never based on anything very deep. We lived on the surface,. and on the surface things didn't seem too bad. But my husband really wanted a stay-at-home wife and being a stay-at-home wife didn't make me happy. I did stop work after I had our first child, but I hated being at home and jumped at the chance of a part-time job where I could take the baby along.

'I don't think my husband had ever got over the difference having a child made. He never got up in the night or offered to lend a hand round the house, even after I started work again. And when I became pregnant (by mistake) the second time he just refused to acknowledge the fact that I was going to have another baby. He just ignored the whole situation. I never intended to have an affair, it was just one of those things that happened. My lover knew all about my pregnancy – I was about three months pregnant when it started – and he was really pleased. He liked the way my body changed, he made me feel good about myself. He did all the things husbands are supposed to do – felt the baby kick, massaged my back. He gave me the love and attention I wasn't getting at home. I don't regret any of it. I was only sad that he couldn't be there when the baby was born. It felt far more like his baby than my husband's.'

Involving your partner in the pregnancy
Generally speaking, though, these kinds of situations are the exception rather than the rule. Many couples find that they can, and do, become closer during pregnancy. The clever woman does her best to involve her man right from the start, encouraging him to read about the changes that are going on as the baby grows, suggesting he goes with her to ante-natal appointments (men who have seen an ultra-sound scan often say this is almost as miraculous and exciting as watching the birth), attending ante-natal classes for fathers-to-be.

One woman said: 'To keep him from feeling left out at first, I used to try to bring him in on everything I bought and asked his advice about what he thought would be best for the baby. We even agreed that I could choose the name if it was a girl and he could if it was a boy.'

It *is* important to get things right at home. You need to come back in the evenings to a man who will, in the words of one woman, 'help with the stress and tension caused by work', not someone who makes you feel under more stress and tension than ever. You may also need his practical help, particularly in the later stages of pregnancy, not just around the house, but in helping you to look the part for work.

When you are working through pregnancy you cannot slop around in the kind of clothes you might wear at home when no one much sees you. If you are going to be efficient, it helps if you look the part. But it is no joke trying to cut and paint your toenails, wash your hair or even put on a pair of tights with a huge bump in front of you. I never dreamed when I got pregnant that I would one day have to ask my husband to perform these intimate tasks for me. But I did, and he did, with humour and love.

And judging by the replies to the survey, he was by no means the only one?

Problems with other relatives
Most of this chapter has dealt with the main relationship at home,

between you and your man, but there are other people to consider too. If you are working through pregnancy, you may find yourself under pressure from other relatives: your parents, his parents, sisters, sisters-in-law.

A buyer said: 'My mother-in-law was horrified when she found out that I intended to carry on working. She even told me I was being thoughtless, that I didn't care about the poor baby and that people would think her son couldn't earn enough to support us! She couldn't understand why I wanted to work when I could have stayed at home knitting bootees. In the end I used to find excuses not to see her. It wasn't worth the hassle.'

If this happens to you there is no point in getting into heated arguments about it. Explain your plans, politely but firmly, and refuse to discuss the situation further. If necessary, cut down the amount of time you spend with people who can't, or won't, see your point of view. Babies have a way of mending bridges when they actually arrive. After all, it is your life. You must decide how to run it.

The single mother
Throughout this chapter I have assumed that life at home includes a man. In fact, some women working through pregnancy will be single mothers. And although I am well aware that in many ways that makes life much harder, it has some compensations too. You won't have someone to take over the cooking, shopping, cleaning. But nor will you have someone else's shirts to iron or meals to prepare.

One woman, who works for a television company, and whose marriage actually broke up just after she discovered she was pregnant, said: 'I got all the emotional support I needed from my colleagues who were marvellous. And the bonus was that there was absolutely no friction at home. I could please myself what I did, when I did it. I didn't have to live up to anyone else's expectations, only my own. I had always been responsible for running the household, so it wasn't a question of missing his help, more a question of having less to do.

'I think that working through pregnancy when you are on your own isn't so bad. It's only later that the going gets tough!'

8
Ante-natal classes

Mrs Smith must have had a hard day at work. She fell asleep during the relaxation exercises.

The law states that a working woman has the right not to be unreasonably refused time off work to receive ante-natal care, and to be paid by her employer for this time. But what is meant by ante-natal care?

Certainly it includes all the hospital or clinic appointments to check the progress of the pregnancy. But the wording could also be interpreted to cover attendance at ante-natal classes in preparation for childbirth. The Maternity Alliance, an independent organization which campaigns for improvements in rights and services for mothers, fathers and babies, admits that this is a very grey area and, as far as they are aware, it is not an issue that has ever been tested by an industrial tribunal.

However, it could be argued that ante-natal classes *are* an important part of ante-natal care, a fact which Sheila Kitzinger is convinced of. She says: 'Good ante-natal care means regular visits to an ante-natal class.'

An employer who does his best to prevent a woman claiming her rights – like the boss who insisted one of his team made all her ante-natal appointments during her lunch hour – is unlikely to agree. However, there are other, more enlightened employers who stick not only to the letter but also to the spirit of the law. And there are others still who are so hazy about the whole business of pregnancy, not to mention maternity rights, that they probably would not notice the difference between a request for time off to go to an ante-natal clinic and one to go to an ante-natal class, especially if the latter is in a hospital.

Ask for time off
Of course, the situation may not arise in every case. Many of the hospital ante-natal classes do not take women who are not already thirty weeks pregnant, and many women stop work at twenty-nine weeks. Others, like those run by National Childbirth Trust teachers, may be held in the evenings as well as during the day. But if the class you want to go to clashes with working hours, it is worth asking for the time off.

When I was working in Fleet Street the only NCT evening class courses either took place too soon in my pregnancy (I thought I would have forgotten it all by the time the baby arrived) or rather late (as it happens, I would have missed the last two classes.) The local hospital classes which were held in the afternoons lasted for seven weeks, and I only had four weeks off work before the expected delivery date. But, to my surprise, when I asked to go to classes during the day, no one raised any objections.

Why go to classes?
There are a number of very good reasons why it is important to go to ante-natal classes, even if you feel there are already enough demands on your time. The only expert I have ever met who disagrees is the famous French obstetrician, Michel Odent, who argues that it is wrong to teach women techniques for coping with labour and birth.

He says: 'At Pithiviers we do just the opposite. On the day of birth we encourage women in labour to give in to the experience, to lose control, to forget all they have learned – all the cultural images, all the behavioural patterns. The less a woman has learned about the "right" way to have a child, the easier it will be for her.'

However, my own ante-natal teacher, Gillian Stellman, who admires much of Michel Odent's work, speaks for many when she says she cannot accept this.

'He is perhaps so strong that he can carry his women through labour. But how many Michel Odents are there? The way I look at it is this: you wouldn't go in for a marathon without preparation. And so it is with childbirth. You need to be physically and mentally prepared.'

Of course, women have given birth for centuries without being taught how to, and if you choose not to go to any classes you will still be able to deliver your baby. Your body will probably respond naturally. But classes are often better than books at helping women to understand the changes that take place in their bodies during pregnancy and labour. If you know what is happening you will be able to work with your body instead of against it and you are more likely to find the birth a satisfying experience. You may find you need less help from the doctors and midwives. You may find you do not need the assistance of drugs to see you through, and if you want a natural birth, rather than a high-tech one, you are more likely to get it if you know the reasons why you are asking for things.

As Gillian points out: 'It's no good saying you don't want syntometrine (a drug given to speed up the delivery of the placenta) if you don't know what it does and the reasons why it may or may not be necessary.'

Making informed decisions

She believes that by going to ante-natal classes you can make an informed choice about the way you would like your labour to progress. Classes can help you sort out in your own mind the things that are most important to you and give you the confidence to ask for them. The vast majority of women give birth in hospital and although there are some who are happy to let the medical staff make all the decisions about the management of labour, many others want to feel that they can be part of the decision-making team.

On the other hand, you need to know what happens during labour before you can take that active role. It may be infuriating to be told not to push when you feel you really want to, for example, but if you know that the anterior lip, or rim of the cervix, has yet to be drawn back past the baby's head and that pushing too soon may make the cervix swell so that the opening becomes smaller instead of bigger, you may find it easier to hold back. Ante-natal classes explain these kinds of things. Being prepared in this way makes most women feel calmer about giving birth.

As Gillian says: 'The more you know, the more you can ask – and the more the midwives will tell you what's going on.' You don't have to be dedicated to the idea of 'natural' childbirth to benefit from knowledge of the physiology of pregnancy and labour. Christine Beels, another teacher, writes in *The Childbirth Book* (Mayflower, 1980):

> Preparation for birth gives us a chance to be knowledgeable and aware, and to at least make an attempt to be in control of our own bodies and any situation we may find ourselves in. The same knowledge which will lead one woman into wanting a conscious drug-free, gentle birth will take another into epidural anaesthesia.'

And she goes on to illustrate this with the example of a labour report from one woman.

> When he said it would be a long time, would I like something to help? I knew what was going on, felt quite happy about it all, and said: 'Yes, could I have an epidural?' Ten or possibly more hours with a posterior lie wasn't what I felt like, although the breathing was going well – I've no complaints about that at all! What a difference it made being able to visualize a posterior baby, nobody else in the ward afterwards even knew what it was, and if I'd had it explained to me then, I don't think I would have been able to take it in properly. . . .

Increasing confidence

Some women say they are not going to go to classes because they do not want to know the nitty-gritty details of what is likely to happen. But if you do not want to think about the reality of the birth itself, you may actually be worried or fearful about it. Fear of the unknown can make you tense, and being tense during pregnancy and labour will affect both you and your baby. Tension and anxiety during pregnancy interferes with the supply of oxygen to your muscles and organs as well as to the growing baby. If you are tense during labour you will have a tendency to contract your muscles and hold your breath. This can slow down your labour so that the stress on you and your baby goes on for longer. In addition, tension makes labour more painful so you may need drugs to cope, and some of these can make your baby drowsy when it is finally born.

By going to classes, learning what happens and ways to cope, you can banish some of the fears and face the birth with more confidence. Classes can also help you find out the truth about all the well-meaning advice you have been given, or help you to put in perspective any of the 'horror' stories you may have been told by people who recently had difficult births.

One woman said: 'I got myself into a bit of a state when I was pregnant because my sister told me, for the first time in detail, about the birth of her baby. It sounded horrendous. She was in labour for more than twenty-four hours and there was a panic at the end. They had to use forceps and she had loads of stitches. I was convinced that it probably ran in families and I was in for a bad time too.

'I finally asked about it at my ante-natal class and came to realize that there was no reason why I was bound to have a long and difficult labour just because my sister had. I came to understand that there were particular problems in her case – the baby was not presenting very well, my sister had been on a foetal monitor from the start and hadn't been allowed to walk or move about, things like that. In the end I went into hospital when my own labour started, feeling much more confident and, in fact, gave birth six hours later with no trouble at all.'

Meeting other mothers

Another good reason for attending ante-natal classes is that they give you an opportunity to meet other women having babies around the same time as yourself. When you are working, particularly if you are working late into your pregnancy, it is often hard to share your enthusiasm or excitement about the baby with colleagues, particularly if they have no children or if they have children who are past the baby stage. They probably won't want to discuss the relative merits of prams or lie-back buggies, and won't be interested in the length of the queues at the local ante-natal clinic. They might want to know if you have chosen a name, but they are less likely to want to know if you are planning to breast or bottle feed.

But other pregnant women form a kind of sisterhood. They will be genuinely interested in swapping experiences. They will sympathize with and encourage your need to focus on the baby as well as on other parts of your life.

A woman who worked as a lab technician said: 'All the people at work were very nice during my pregnancy. They asked all the right questions: did I want a boy or a girl, could I feel the baby moving yet, which hospital was I going to, was my husband going to be with me at the birth? But I couldn't really talk to them in the way I could talk to the other women in my class. Just about everything came up, from how hard it was to make love with a bump to whether we were worried about being cut or torn during delivery.

I'd worked for the same lab for six years and had made some good friends there. But in the eight weeks I went to the classes I think I got closer to some of the women than I had been to anyone since I made friends at school.'

Support after the baby is born

The friendships that can form in this way not only play an important supporting role during pregnancy, but can gell into a network of support after the baby is born.

Unless your home is in a closely-knit community, or you live in the same area where you grew up, the chances are that as a working woman you know relatively few people locally. You may be friendly with your immediate neighbours, be on nodding terms with those a few doors away. You may recognize the ones who wait at the same bus stop every morning, or catch the same train. But how many women do you know who are at home near you during the day?

If you are planning to stay at home with your baby, whether for a few months or indefinitely, the early days can prove to be very lonely. Most of us take for granted the kind of companionship we have at work, even if we do not have close friends there. Once you stop work you may need something to fill that gap. Even if you find you have plenty to do in the weeks before the baby is born, afterwards can be another matter.

However delightful you find your new baby, there will almost certainly be times when you think you will go mad if the only person you speak to all day is the milkman or the lady at the supermarket check-out. And if you happen to find yourself with a baby who is driving you up the wall, you will need to share your problems with someone who understands. Just having somewhere else to go, someone else's kitchen to drink coffee in, can be a help.

These days, relatively few of us have an extended family close to hand – mothers, sisters, aunts, cousins, or in-laws who are willing to listen or lend a hand. Even if your nearest female relatives do live nearby, they themselves may be out at work.

Making new friends is not always easy, but even if the baby is the only thing you seem to have in common at first, there are friends to be made through ante-natal classes.

Helping each other out
If you intend to work fairly soon after the birth of your child you may think that making contact with other local mothers is not particularly important. If you take this attitude though, you are cutting yourself off from a source of moral and emotional support that you may find useful. A network of local mothers can prove useful in other ways too, not least when it comes to borrowing equipment that is not worth buying because you only need it now and then. For example, one of the friends I made at ante-natal classes owns a travel cot that I have gratefully borrowed a number of times.

You can also get together with other mothers to set up an informal babysitting circle. And there are times when even the best and most organized child-care arrangements go wrong. The working mum always needs some kind of emergency back-up. A friend who knows your baby and understands just what a child of that age needs can be a real boon on the days when the childminder is ill or your Scottish nanny is stranded in Glasgow because of a rail strike.

What kind of class?

Having, I hope, persuaded you that it is worth finding the time to attend ante-natal classes, the next question is: What kind of class?

Generally speaking, there will be two different types of ante-natal classes in your area: those run by the hospital, or perhaps, by local health centres or clinics, and those run by organizations such as the National Childbirth Trust. There may also be yoga-based exercise classes (see chapter 5) or classes run by local birth centre teachers.

It pays to do your homework before you book in, and to carry out your enquiries at a fairly early stage in pregnancy so you can be sure of getting a place. You can opt for more than one class if you want to. If you have the time and the energy, there is nothing to stop you doing hospital classes, NCT classes and yoga classes, since all can complement each other in different ways.

Finding out about classes

However, if you decide to choose one kind rather than another, it is a good idea to consider a variety of different aspects. Ask about the classes before you sign on. Glean information not just from the teachers but from women who have already completed the courses and had their babies. If you have not got any local contracts among the neighbourhood mothers, you can at least ask the other women you meet at the ante-natal clinic. Not all will be first-time mothers. Some will have been to classes last time round.

Ask how much information was given, and how easy it was to understand. Were you allowed to ask questions? Were questions answered properly or was the attitude one of 'you don't really need to know that'? Find out if women were taught exercises to help them relax or techniques to cope with labour and, equally important, whether any of these helped when they were in labour.

Just because a woman ends up having a difficult labour or needs help with the birth, this does not necessarily mean that the classes she went to were no help at all. Having a baby is not like taking an exam: even with the best coaching in the world you may still have a tough time. But many women who have had difficult deliveries still say that going to the right classes helped. Compare these two accounts, both given by women who ended up having their babies by Caesarian section. The first woman said:

'After eight hours of pretty strong contractions it was fairly obvious we were not getting anywhere. My cervix was just not dilating. Towards the end they had put me on a monitor and eventually the doctor told me he thought it would be best for me and the baby if they did a Caesarian. I had managed quite well up to then with my breathing, but I also felt that I had just about had it, especially since nothing was happening. So I agreed. I was sorry not to have a normal birth but I accepted that that was just the way things had turned out.

'I was glad I had been to classes because I knew what was – or wasn't! – happening and I think because I was able to ask the right kind of questions, everyone was very good about explaining everything to me. I can't say I really enjoyed the experience, but it wasn't a complete nightmare either.'

This is what happened to the second woman.

'I suppose I had a pretty naive approach to it all. I thought however awful it was, it would soon be over and that the hospital would give me something if the pain got too bad. They did give me some pethidine, but it didn't really take the pain away, just made me a bit woozy which didn't really help. I couldn't understand why it seemed to be taking so long. No one really explained anything to me. They came and checked the monitor and did some internal examinations and then they said they wanted to do a Caesarian because the baby was showing signs of distress. I got very panicky than as I thought the baby was going to die, but of course, he didn't.

'I was torn between wanting them to do something to get it all over and fear of being put to sleep to have an operation. All in all, it was a horrible experience, not at all the way I'd imagined it. I can't imagine ever having another baby.'

What a good class should do

This second account illustrates why it is important to find out about the content of the classes. Good classes will explain the mechanics of pregnancy and childbirth and help you to understand the changes going on in your body and the sequence of events during labour and birth. They will teach you how to recognize the signs that labour has started, or is about to start (not always as obvious as it would seem), and help you decide when it is time to call the midwife or go to the hospital.

They will discuss the ways in which labour progresses and the ways you can cope. They should show you some exercises in breathing and relaxation and give you plenty of opportunity to practise these. They should also be able to suggest different positions which you might want to use during labour and delivery. Lying flat on your back is not the best position because the weight of your uterus on the major blood vessels in your back reduces the blood-flow and hence the supply of oxygen to the baby, and your uterus is also working against the force of gravity.

Some positions and techniques can help you to speed up a labour or encourage the contractions to become stronger and more efficient, some are useful if you are feeling most of the pain in your back, and others may help you to slow down a labour that seems to be going too fast.

A good class will also discuss the emotional changes that you may undergo during pregnancy and, more particularly, labour, and suggest ways in which your husband or birth partner can help by giving both physical and moral support.

Classes should also cover the kind of hospital procedures you might face during labour, from admission and preparation (some hospitals still routinely shave and give enemas) to ways in which your labour may be induced or accelerated. The use of different kinds of drugs for pain relief should be discussed, as well as other techniques used in the management of labour, from the artificial rupturing of the membranes, to foetal monitoring, episiotomy and Caesarian sections.

Comparing local choices

There are other advantages and disadvantages to consider. When I had my daughter, both the local maternity hospital where I was booked and NCT teachers in the area ran classes. I went to both and was therefore able to draw direct comparisons. Since then little has changed, although the hospital classes are now held in the far more luxurious surroundings of the new ante-natal department, and I feel sure that my experience reflects fairly accurately the situation elsewhere in the country.

The first thing to consider is the question of timing, which has already been mentioned. Hospital classes are held during the day which is difficult if you are still working, and, even if you have stopped work by the time the course starts, your partner is likely to be working and therefore unlikely to be able to attend. NCT hold day time classes but there are nearly always evening classes as well. Check, too, whether your own doctor runs classes, as those can be very good and may be at a time you can manage.

Then there is the question of cost. Hospital classes are free. At the moment, the fees for a course of NCT classes varies quite widely depending on your area. But because the NCT is a charity, it operates a fee-waiving system, so if you cannot afford to pay you won't have to.

The size of the group

At my local hospital, about forty women are usually booked for classes at the same time. They are split into two groups. Gillian's classes are usually no bigger than eight.

The size of a group does make a difference. In a small group it is easier to build up a relationship with the teacher, to get your own questions answered, to share experiences, worries, ideas. I certainly found NCT classes far less formal. We sat on the floor or on large cushions in someone else's front room, rather than on standard issue NHS chairs ranged round a room in the hospital. There was less of a feeling of 'them and us'. Gillian talked with us, not to us. Going to hospital classes felt rather like going back to school. NCT classes were more like a coffee morning with a purpose. As Gillian put it: 'I see myself more as a group leader, than a lecturer.'

Because each NCT class was longer than a hospital class, it was possible to cover topics in more depth. With the hospital classes there was the distinct feeling that a particular number of subjects was going to be covered each week and that the timetable had to be stuck to. And because it was harder for the hospital staff to get to know the women in the group personally, it was impossible for them to know how much basic knowledge, if any, each woman had. They had, in effect, to assume that no one really knew anything.

Gillian, on the other hand, was able to match the classes to the individual group. And while she always aims to cover all the necessary topics, the order in which she does this can vary. As she puts it: 'If someone raises a question about epidurals in the very first class, it's no good my saying we'll discuss it in class six. She wants to know then and there.'

Are the teachers well trained?
Another point to bear in mind is how well trained the different teachers are. The National Childbirth Trust has been running classes for pregnant women for thirty years. Teachers take an average of two years to train during which time they attend tutorials, read a lot, write essays, go to weekend seminars, sit in on two sets of classes and work out class plans. Each teacher has to re-register each year and is supervised every two years to make sure she is keeping up with current information and trends. Classes in hospitals are usually run by midwives and/or physiotherapists and the quality of the teaching can vary enormously depending on the individual women and the hospital policy. In some hospitals the classes are run so haphazardly that any midwife who is free may be called up from the labour ward to take a class.

On the other hand, the NCT has been asked, in some areas, to run courses for health professionals who take ante-natal classes, not to teach them about anatomy and so on, but how to run a group.

Using the time to best advantage
It may sound like I believe there is nothing to be gained by going to a hospital rather than an NCT class. In fact, this is not the case. Certainly I feel that with most hospital classes there is room for improvement. Many of them, like the ones I went to, spent quite a lot of time on aspects of parentcraft. We were shown how to fold and change nappies, we were given a doll on which to practise bathing, topping and tailing and changing. We were also shown how to sterilize bottles and make up a baby's feed.

It seemed to me a waste of time that could more profitably have been spent on other topics. First-time mothers generally stay in hospital for several days after the birth of their babies. The staff on the post-natal ward will cover all this ground, and it is far more valuable practising on your own baby than it is on a doll.

Even if you are only going to be in hospital for forty-eight hours or less, you will be visited at home by the community midwife and perhaps your GP or health visitor, who can give you the kind of information you might need. It is not the end of the world if you cannot fold a nappy – more and more women are using disposable nappies anyway. And the tins of powdered baby milk carry instructions for use on them. Breastfeeding is another matter, but it is something you can only learn by doing it. And once again, it seems to me, this is where the NCT wins hands down.

Every area has its own breastfeeding counsellor who will come to one of the NCT classes before the birth. When you get home, she will be available to give you practical advice and moral support in a way that the health professionals may not have time to. The hospital classes may also attempt to give you some idea what life will be like after the baby and to convince you of the importance of looking after yourself, getting enough rest and so on. The NCT can, once again, provide something more concrete in terms of post-natal support groups and counsellors.

Getting to know the hospital
Probably the two main advantages of hospital classes are that they enable you to familiarize yourself with the hospital and some of the staff and that through them you get some idea of the hospital's attitudes to things like pain relief, the length of an ideal labour, and positions for delivery.

At the second of the series of seven classes at my local hospital, for example, women are taken on a tour of the maternity hospital and are able to see for themselves where they should check-in, where they will probably spend most of their labour and where they will deliver their babies. Of course, an increasing number of women ask to see round a hospital before they decide to book into it, but this is usually done in the early stages of pregnancy and a second look much nearer the time of the birth is well worthwhile, since, by then, you will probably have a much clearer idea of what you hope will happen.

The people who give the classes may well be some of those you will meet once you are admitted. Some of the student midwives who were present at my hospital classes later turned up on the delivery and post-natal wards, and it was nice to see some familiar faces. The physiotherapist who gave relaxation instruction also turned up after the birth to talk about post-natal exercises.

If you want to find out about the hospital's attitudes to various aspects of childbirth, you will have to use the time available during the classes to ask questions and learn to interpret some of the things that are said.

Whatever your own views, do be sure to elicit information in an unaggressive way, otherwise you will simply alienate the professionals who may, justifiably, believe they know more about the business of delivering babies than you do. This is not to say that you have to accept or agree with everything they say, but you are more likely to get the maximum information about what really goes on if the person you are asking does not immediately label you a know-it-all or a troublemaker.

What questions should you ask?
Some of the questions you might like to ask include:
1. How many women have drugs for pain relief, such as pethidine, epidurals, or Entonox?
2. How long do you allow women to continue in labour without deciding to try to speed things up? How would you usually do this – by artificially rupturing the membranes, or by an oxytocin drip?
3. How long do most women take in the second, pushing stage?
4. How many women are put on a foetal monitoring machine? How do they decide when this is necessary?
5. How many women have episiotomies?
6. Do most women move around in the first stages of labour? If so, where can they walk?
7. What is the most common position for women to give birth in? What other positions are used?

You can learn a lot from the way in which the replies to your questions are answered. There is a world of difference between a hospital where a midwife says: 'Most women give birth in a sitting position, propped up by extra pillows. But some women find it more comfortable kneeling or squatting or lying on their side', and one where she says: 'Most women give birth in a sitting position, propped up by extra pillows. But some women seem to think they are going to get on better if they squat or kneel.'

Advantages in different classes
If I had to make the choice between hospital classes and those run

by the NCT or similar groups, I would go for the latter. But, as I said earlier, the two groups are not mutally exclusive and can complement each other. A teacher who went to NCT classes and those run by her local hospital said: 'The NCT classes helped enormously by teaching me about pregnancy and labour and ways to make things easier on myself. Because I was able to go to the classes with my husband, we felt very close, we were really able to share everything including the birth. It made it *our* baby right from the start.

'The hospital classes were useful in a different way. I think the kind of relaxation techniques and exercises that they suggested were pretty useless and I wouldn't have liked to have relied on them, but I did feel I got to know more about the maternity unit and the people who ran it.

'When we bowled up in the middle of the night everything felt very familiar which was comforting. I knew where I was going to go and what was going to happen to me once I got inside those doors. And I knew that while there wouldn't be a problem about some of the things I hoped for, I might have to be firm about others.

'I'd already decided there was no point making a fuss about having a shave and an enema and I was reassured to know that they didn't routinely give all women episisotomies. But I was a bit worried about the number of women who seemed to be given pethidine, which was something I wanted to avoid. One of the midwives did, in fact, try to persuade me to "have something to take the pain away" because in her view the labour was going to go on for quite a long time and I would be too tired to push properly. As it happens, the baby was born less than two hours later and I was really pleased I'd stuck to my guns as I knew that pethidine given less than three hours before delivery can have an effect on the baby.'

It is usually quite easy to find out what kind of ante-natal classes are on offer in your area. The NHS classes are run either by the hospital, in which case they will tell you about them when you book in, or by your GP, the local health centre, local midwives or health visitors. You can find out where your nearest NCT teacher is by contacting the headquarters in London and if there is a local Birth Centre, they might run classes too.

Finally, if you really cannot spare the time to get to classes, despite all the benefits they can give you, you can at least prepare yourself as much as possible by reading up on the subject.

9
A second baby

> How would you like a little brother or sister to play with?

> I'd rather have a new bike

Many of the books about pregnancy and childbirth pay scant attention to the possibility that the women who are reading them may well be having their second or even their third baby. If they do acknowledge the fact, it is often only in passing or in a section which deals with ways to break the news to your first child that he is going to have a new brother or sister.

Yet these days an increasing number of women go back to work after having a baby and many of these will still be working through their next pregnancy. When I became pregnant for the second time I faced the months ahead with far more confidence than I had the first time round, but I was also aware of new questions and new doubts.

When I turned to my reference books for advice, little was forthcoming. Only the redoubtable Sheila Kitzinger, in her book *Pregnancy and Childbirth,* came close to putting into words some of the things I was feeling.

> Pregnancy the second or third time round is a new experience. It will not be exactly like the first time. It holds different challenges. Coping with them involves flexibility and resourcefulness on the part of both parents. In some ways things are much easier because you know what to expect and have probably developed self-confidence in your role as childbearer. You may sail through pregnancy with style and thoroughly enjoy it. But there may be difficulties which come as a surprise because you thought that everything would be simple this time.

However, even Sheila Kitzinger's second-time mum seems to have a lifestyle far removed from that of the average working woman. During her first pregnancy, according to Sheila Kitzinger, she was able to luxuriate in afternoon rests with time for thinking, planning and dreaming. During the second, her main concerns are ferrying children to and from school, cooking and cleaning.

With all this to contend with, she suggests, your second pregnancy may run a poor second to your other commitments as 'wife, mother, nurse, psychotherapist, teacher, hostess, house cleaner, chief cook and bottle washer' and you may feel guilty that you are not giving the new baby the time or love you gave the first.

If the non-working mother feels this way, then pity the working mother who has all these tasks plus a job to hold down. As one woman, who managed to juggle the demands of a full time job, a large house, a workaholic husband and a two-year old, said: 'I probably would have felt guilty about the baby, if only I'd had the time!'

Knowing the problems

Working through a second pregnancy *can* be easier in some respects than working through a first, if only because the changes that take place within your body have a certain familiarity. The first time round you may have learnt how to pace yourself, how to sort out the priorities in your daily life. One woman who worked as the assistant to a marketing manager said: 'During my first pregnancy I was determined to keep up with the work. If that meant staying late sometimes, then that's what I did. But I got very tired and I don't think it was good for me or the department. The second time I was a lot tougher. I learned to say "no" sometimes, especially on occasions when it didn't really matter if a report was copied and circulated at the end of one day or the beginning of another. And I also learned to delegate more. Instead of taking reports round myself, I used to get the office junior to do it.'

During the second pregnancy you may still suffer from the same problems, like morning sickness, but by this time you will know the best ways of dealing with it, A teacher said: 'I was just as sick the second time but at least I knew ways of keeping it under control. I knew I had to get up at least half an hour earlier in the morning – if I had to rush things were much worse. And during the first pregnancy I'd found that if I nibbled at digestive biscuits on and off all day, it kept the feeling of nausea at bay a little. So I never went anywhere without my packet of biscuits.

'And even when I was hanging over the loo in the staff toilets I was at least able to comfort myself that this stage wasn't going to last for ever. First time round I couldn't imagine a time when I wasn't going to feel sick.'

Different complications

On the other hand, a second pregnancy can be very different from a first, and may produce different discomforts or complications. You may even find you look pregnant far earlier second time round. A translator said: 'With my first baby I was able to wear ordinary clothes until I was almost five months pregnant. The second time I definitely looked pregnant at three months. My stomach behaved rather like a balloon – having been blown up once, it went quicker the next time!' Far from being delighted with her changing shape, in the way that many first-time mothers are, the second-time mother may hate the idea of having to get back into her maternity clothes. A secretary said: 'The first time I was pregnant I could hardly wait to rush out and buy myself some real maternity clothes. But I was sick of them by the time the baby was born and the worst thing was that they were still the only things that fitted me for a while afterwards. When I got pregnant for the second time, I could hardly bear the thought of getting them out again.'

New clothes

Your morale is an important factor in any pregnancy and if you feel good about the way you look you are bound to be in a better frame of mind to tackle the tasks you have to do, at work and at home. If you have a perfectly good set of maternity clothes in your wardrobe it would be an extravagant gesture to throw them out and replace them with a set of new ones, but I do not think it is indulgent to buy a few things. Perhaps you could get one new outfit to cover those early, difficult months when zips won't do up and blouses won't button, and another for the last month or so when you feel positively elephantine.

If you really feel guilty about spending money on new clothes, or if the budget just will not stretch to it, see if you can borrow some instead. As a second-time mother you are more likely to be in touch with other mothers than you were when you were expecting your first baby, and it is unlikely that they will all be pregnant at exactly the same time as you. And speaking as someone who has cheerfully rifled through other women's wardrobes, I know that they are usually only to happy to lend things that are just taking up space, providing you look after them and return them clean. It certainly makes a big difference to wear something 'new'.

Worries about the birth

Clothes may seem a trivial problem if you are worrying about something far more important – the birth itself. And if your first labour and delivery was not a satisfying experience, you may have some real fears on this score. Far from having the confidence that most people expect from a second-time mother, you may actually be more concerned about what is going to happen than you were first time round.

An accounts clerk said: 'With my first baby I was sublimely confident. I was young, I was healthy, I went to all the ante-natal clinic appointments, millions of women had babies and I couldn't imagine there was anything to make a fuss about. I didn't read up about it much. I didn't bother about breathing exercises or anything because I was going to have an epidural and I thought that meant there wouldn't be any pain.

'However, when I got to the hospital in labour and asked for one it turned out that the anaesthetist was not available and I had to manage without. It was terrible. The pain was so bad I wanted to die. I didn't have a clue what was happening, how long it would all go on. I made a real exhibition of myself.

'When I got pregnant again I could hardly bear to think about the birth. I got into a real state about it. It affected everything: the way I coped at work, the way I behaved at home. I was tense and snappy. I wanted the baby but I was scared of actually having it. This time, though, towards the end of the pregnancy, I went to a course of NCT classes and they helped a lot. Not only did they teach me what kinds of things to expect, and how I could help myself, but I was able to talk about the way I felt and it was good to be able to confront my fears. And the birth itself went even better than I'd hoped. This time there was no feeling of panic, and though it certainly wasn't pain-free, it was bearable and even, oddly satisfying.'

The National Childbirth Trust – and some hospitals – run special refresher courses for second-time mothers. The hospital ones, for instance, tend to skip the parentcraft bit and concentrate on relaxation and breathing exercises.

Gillian Stellman, my own NCT ante-natal teacher, runs a series of three refresher classes (compared to the eight classes for first-time mums) to revise the relaxation exercises, to discuss the first-time birth experiences and also to deal with the practicalities of coping with more than one child.

Ante-natal classes

In the previous chapter I discussed the various reasons why it is important for a working mum-to-be to find time to go to ante-natal classes, and even if you have no particular fears about the forthcoming birth, it is still a good idea to do this in a second pregnancy. You may not have forgotten all you learnt about the physiology of childbirth, but you may not remember it all in detail either. In addition, hospital practices may have changed, and attitudes to drugs or techniques used in childbirth may have altered as more information has become available.

I found that some ideas had changed in the two and a half years between the births of my two children, for example. In 1981, although my NCT teacher talked about the desirability of giving birth in practically any position except lying flat on your back, there was more emphasis on supported sitting positions than on squatting, kneeling or anything else. And the local hospital midwife flatly refused to deliver me when I was in a kneeling position because 'I won't be able to see what's happening if everything is upside down'.

By 1984, the NCT classes discussed all the possibilities in detail and the midwives at the hospital had obviously learned the knack of 'upside down' births, because they raised no objections to women wanting to deliver on all fours.

The reactions of other people

It is one thing to discover that the attitudes of the health professionals have changed, but quite another to realize that the attitudes of workmates, friends and even your husband are different towards you during a second working pregnancy.

A researcher said: 'To start with I think my boss was a bit put out when she realized I was going to want to take another period of maternity leave, although she never actually said it would cause problems. And generally, people at work just were not so interested. Maybe a first baby is more of an event, even for yourself, and somehow your feelings are picked up by those around you. But although everyone was very nice and I had no trouble getting time off when necessary, there just wasn't the same level of concern. I wasn't made to feel so special.'

Some women reported that they were under more pressure from relatives to stop working during the second pregnancy. A shop assistant who had gone back to work part-time said: 'My mother tried to persuade me to stop work almost as soon as we told her I was pregnant again.

'She said that she understood why I had worked for the twenty-nine weeks in my first pregnancy – we needed the money and there was really no reason to stop – but now that my husband was earning more she felt we could manage without my money and she thought I was taking on too much.

'I tried to explain that I liked the job and that it made a big difference to me to get out of the house for a while three days a week and that I liked having some money of my own. A neighbour used to look after my little boy when I worked, but I felt that once the new baby arrived I would probably have to give up work for quite a while as there was no way I could ask her to take two. So I just wanted to carry on as long as I could.

'But Mum either couldn't or wouldn't understand. She kept on saying I'd tire myself out. In fact, looking after a boisterous two-year-old was far more tiring than helping out in a shop!'

A less supportive husband

It is even possible that your husband may be less supportive second time round. A computer programmer said: 'When we first got married we shared all the chores and during my first pregnancy my husband did more than his share, if anything. But once I'd left work to have the baby it did seem to make sense, since I was the one at home, for me to take over most of the household tasks, including cleaning, shopping and ironing.

'The trouble was that even after I went back to work. I still seemed to be responsible for most of these things. Even if he offered to do the shopping, I had to make a list for him. I was the one who looked after the baby's clothes and it did seem petty not to do my husband's washing and ironing at the same time. So we never really got the balance the same again.

'During the first pregnancy I never had to ask him to do anything, he was the one rushing round with the vacuum cleaner telling me to put my feet up when I came in from work. During the second pregnancy he did, admittedly, take over some of the cooking without being asked, and he used to bath our daughter and put her to bed, but he also used to say things like 'are there any clean shirts' or 'why haven't we got any bread?' He seemed to take it for granted that I would just sail on the same as ever.

'He wasn't as excited about the baby either. The first time, he used to like sitting with his hand on my tummy to feel the baby kick. He read all the books I had about pregnancy and came to classes with me. But the second time he was much more matter-of-fact. I can remember lying in bed, unable to sleep because it felt as if the baby was turning somersaults inside me. I must have disturbed him because he woke up and asked me what the matter was.

'When I told him he just said "oh", turned over and went back to sleep. But the first time round he would have wanted to feel my tummy going up and down. This time, I suppose, it wasn't so much of a novelty.'

Discussing the pregnancy with your husband

This kind of response can be upsetting, and it is a good idea to talk to your husband about the feeling you both have about the pregnancy and the forthcoming new baby. You may not be able to alter the attitudes of others, such as people at work, or other members of your family (although being prepared for their reactions may help you to deal with them), but with the extra demands that working through a pregnancy brings, it is important to have a sound base of understanding at home.

Research carried out in Britain and America shows that the arrival of children causes the level of marital satisfaction to drop sharply. In her book *Marriage* (Fontana, 1983), Maureen Green writes:

> ... the arrival of a first baby, regarded among friends and family as a source of joy and celebration, conceals for many an agonizing revolution, in which the positive and satisfying bits are brought out into public view to be a matter for congratulation and the negative, frightening and oppressive parts are carefully hidden from view, and even denied by the couple themselves.

Having a baby can cause all kinds of stresses within a relationship. A husband may feel excluded, pushed into second place by his wife's love for the child. A wife, particularly a working wife, may feel angry and resentful if she does not get the back-up at home that she feels she needs. These kinds of emotional time-bombs, if not defused, can go on quietly ticking away until a second pregnancy sets off an explosion.

If you feel different

One woman said: 'During my first pregnancy everything was wonderful. I felt incredibly sexy all the time and our love-life was fantastic. It was so good that my husband couldn't wait to pick up where we'd left off, after the baby was born. At first he put my lack of response down to tiredness, but as the months went by he became less and less understanding. I did feel tired, but I felt emotionally drained, too. I felt everybody wanted something

A SECOND BABY

from me. I was giving – to him, and to the baby, and not getting much back.

'While I was off on maternity leave I naturally did most of the domestic chores, including most of the child care. And for the first six months I was the one who had the broken nights. At first, because I was breastfeeding, it was obviously going to have to be me who got up when the baby cried. But later on, when I started to wean her and when, anyway, she wasn't waking up for food, it was still me who went, as my husband said he had to get up and go to work the next morning.

'But when my leave ended and I went back to work, it was still me who woke up when she cried, still me who got up to see what the matter was. I was the one who had to get up that bit earlier to get the baby up, while my husband had a leisurely shave and bath. And I was the one who had to get home on time to see the baby before she went to bed. I used to say that it was a lot easier being a father than a mother – you got all the fun and not much of the hassle.

'We'd agreed that we wanted two children and when our little girl was two we decided to try for another baby. It had taken me quite a long time to get pregnant the first time, so it was rather a surprise to fall straight away. We were both pleased, but for different reasons. My husband made no bones about it. He said he hoped I'd be as sexy this time as I had been the last.

'Of course, I wasn't. The first time I'd been on a high of triumph and anticipation. This time I knew what things were going to be like. And when I'd got in from work, put our daughter to bed and cobbled together some kind of meal, the last thing I wanted to do was make mad, passionate love.'

Another woman, whose second pregnancy was accidental, says her husband flatly refused to discuss it. 'He had never really adjusted to the changes that having one child had meant. He was never prepared to share any of the extra load at home. What he really wanted was a stay-at-home wife who would have his slippers ready and his meal waiting. I did try to involve myself in the domestic role, baking bread and all that kind of thing. But when I had the chance to go back to work part-time I jumped at it. By the time I found I was pregnant again I had a full-time job. I just had to cope with everything. He ignored the fact I was pregnant.'

Sorting out marital problems

Not surprisingly, this marriage ultimately ended in divorce, but many other couples find a way of facing up to the differences of hopes and expectations that having children bring. A second pregnancy gives them the impetus to examine the relationship and to work out how to survive as a family.

The woman whose second pregnancy was not as sexually rewarding as her husband had hoped said: 'Things got quite black and in desperation I went to see a marriage guidance counsellor. I had to wait six weeks before the appointment, which seemed ages but I gather wasn't that long compared to some areas, and I didn't know how much help it would be. But even though my husband wouldn't come with me, I was able to sort things out in my mind and come home and talk, rather than yell at him or push him away.

'We both tried harder. We got our priorities sorted out. I began to see that although I resented the fact that he hadn't been helping at nights and so on, I had under-estimated the kind of moral support he had to offer in other ways. We both had to learn to stop thinking of our individual needs and to work together as a unit, as a family.'

Tiredness

Of course any difficulty, however large or small, seems that much harder to tackle if your mind is dulled and your body aches with fatigue. And feeling tired all the time is a common complaint of many women working through a second pregnancy.

In some ways this is not surprising, since the burden of looking after an older child is added to the list of things to cope with. A sales agent with a large airline, who worked for thirty-three weeks during her first pregnancy, but stopped at twenty-nine weeks with her second, said: 'My first pregnancy was a continual battle against high blood pressure, which eventually stopped me from working as long as I would have liked. However, I felt perfectly well.

'My second pregnancy had no such problems. My blood pressure was normal throughout. Yet this time I felt awful. Second time round, I found work much more of a strain, probably because I already had another child to look after. It was very tiring coping with a two-year-old, work and pregnancy. This is why I decided to take the maximum maternity leave available to me.'

A civil servant, who also had a two-year-old, said: 'The second time I felt too physically tired to enjoy working, but we needed the money.' And a local government officer, who had a three-year-old, added: 'I didn't enjoy work so much the second time because I had an older child to look after. And when I did stop work at thirty-three weeks, I was too tired to enjoy being with her.'

Another civil servant made the point that it is not just the time you spend looking after a child, instead of resting, that can tire you out, but the sheer effort involved in arranging for someone else to care for that child when you are at work. She went back to work when her first baby was five and a half months old, and became pregnant again when he was two.

She said: 'The second time I only managed because I worked flexible hours. On a bad day I could go in late and come home early. Then on a good day I could put in extra hours. The hard part was travelling. I took my first child with me, on the bus. I had his pushchair, a bag and I was also pregnant.

'He enjoyed the travel, we became well-known on the bus, but I found it very tiring.'

Changing your work pattern

On the other hand, some women found that they were actually *less* tired during their second pregnancy than they had been during their first. There were a number of reasons for this. To begin with, many women alter their working patterns once they have a child. Those who return to work may choose to work part-time, often in a different capacity, but in a job that is nearer to home. The journey itself may not be so tiring or, if circumstances have changed, they may be able to drive the family car to work rather than relying on public transport, which is considerably less exhausting than queuing for a bus in the rain or strap-hanging in the tube.

Nurses, in particular, seem able to rearrange their working hours to fit in with their responsibilities as mothers. One nursery nurse in a maternity hospital said: 'I went back to the same job but only doing part-time (twenty hours). When I became pregnant again I found it easier at work. I felt less tired and seemed to have more energy even though I had a toddler to look after.'

Others went back to working part-time night shifts, which meant that husbands *had* to do their share. In fact, many women reported that husbands were actually more helpful during the second pregnancy than they had been during the first.

An office worker said: 'I think my husband was keener to help this time as he enjoyed spending the time with our first child, while I put my feet up. He used to get her to help him prepare the meals and put the washing on and they had a nice time together.

'We both felt it was important because she had always been a bit of a mummy's girl and we worried about her reaction to the new baby. This way, her relationship with her father blossomed and I don't think it was quite so much of a shock having to share me after the baby was born. There was someone else she could happily turn to.'

I myself found it easier working through a second pregnancy because like many women, I had adjusted my work pattern to suit my home life. Instead of travelling in to Fleet Street every day, I was based at home, which was less tiring. But in order to work at all I had had to employ Jan, a full-time live-in nanny. When I became pregnant again I did not have to cope with a toddler in the evenings if I did not feel up to it. I certainly didn't have to worry about keeping her in clean clothes. And because Jan had agreed to take on most of the housework when my cleaning lady had left, there were relatively few chores to worry about.

She didn't mind adding my dirty linen to the nursery wash. She even took over my ironing, fed me at lunchtimes and made sure there was enough left-overs for my husband at night. And on top of all this she nagged me to put my feet up for an hour at lunchtimes and deftly fielded all business calls which came through while I was resting.

Saving effort on the domestic front

However, I know that for most women this kind of help and support is a luxury that is only to be dreamed about. Most women working through a second pregnancy have to help themselves. In chapter 7 I discussed various ways in which women can lighten the domestic load, and if this advice is worth taking during a first working pregnancy, then it is doubly so during a second.

Things like cutting the housework down to a minimum,

getting your husband to do his share, investing in labour-saving devices, making the most of delivery services, and paying for help in the home, can all make working through a second pregnancy more enjoyable. But there may be other things you want to consider, too.

The biggest difference this time round is that you have another child to care for, another person making demands on your time and energy, doubling the load of washing, putting sticky fingers over the furniture, dropping juice and cereal on the kitchen floor, needing to be fed, washed, played with. At first it might seem an impossible task to reduce the workload produced by one small person, but there are ways.

As a working mother you probably know the value of easy-care clothes. Now is the time to be ruthless. Don't buy anything new for your child that cannot be machine-washed and drip-dried or tumble-dried. If he or she already has clothes that need to be handwashed or ironed, put them away if at all possible.

Spending time with your first child
You may find you need to reorganize the time you spend with your child or the use you make of it. If he or she is cared for by a childminder during the day, for instance, perhaps it would suit you better to collect your offspring a little later.

A VDU operator who had a three-year-old and continued to work in her second pregnancy until the thirty-first week, said: 'Before I was pregnant again I used to pick my little boy up from the childminder on the way home from work, then I'd give him his tea and his bath, and we'd play a little before bedtime.

'But I found that I was really tired by the time I got us both home and I was very short-tempered with him. After a while I asked the childminder whether she would mind giving him his tea. This meant I could go straight home and have a bath myself or have a bit of a rest with a cup of tea before going to collect him.

'At first I felt a bit guilty about leaving him for another hour, but I have to say that it worked much better for both of us. He was happier once he'd had his tea and I felt much more able to cope with him after I'd had a bit of time to myself to unwind. Even though I had less time with him in the evening , I think we both enjoyed it more.'

You probably won't have the energy for rough-and-tumble games so now is the time to think of things you can do quietly together. Sitting down to read books is ideal, but not all children will co-operate. But what about story tapes, or video cassettes?

In fact, if you own a video recorder, it is a good idea to set the timer to record some of the children's programmes during the day, which you can then watch with your child in the evening.

Sedentary pastimes

Anything that can be done while you sit or lie down is worth a try. Painting is probably out (too much mess to clear up) but cutting and sticking, particularly if you use gummed paper, is possible. So is crayoning, or doing jigsaw puzzles, or playing simple games like picture dominoes or snap.

You could teach an older child to knit (yes, even boys) or play I-Spy or draughts. If you have an imaginative child who likes playing pretend games, you can play doctors and nurses (you are the patient, of course), or you can send them off on 'shopping trips' or get them to 'cook' you breakfast in bed. The point of the exercise is to get them to wear off their surplus energy while you sit with your feet up on the sofa.

One of my friends used to make bath-time and extended water-play session. She said: 'I used to give my toddler all kinds of things to play with – empty yoghurt pots, straws, the plastic teaset, little boats, bathable dolls. I used to sit on a big wicker chair with my feet up on the side of the bath so I could keep an eye on her but she was generally quite happy playing by herself for a good forty minutes, while I relaxed. Sometimes, before I got too huge, I used to get in with her myself.'

Another friend used to keep a small cardboard box handy into which she dropped interesting odds and ends as she found them. 'Just junk really, but things that would amuse a two-year-old. Empty egg boxes, cotton reels and a shoelace for threading. Some of that bubble cellophane packaging that can be popped. Leaflets advertising Disneyworld with pictures of Mickey Mouse. The inner tubes from rolls of kitchen foil.' Every so often, when I really needed to keep her quiet so I could rest up, I'd tell her that if she was good she could have the Treasure Box.'

An older child might be given a button box to sort through, or be allowed to look at Mummy's jewellery box. If, like me, you have hundreds of photographs that you have never quite got round to sticking in an album, you might find that your child will be happy to sit down next to you while you sort through them together. This is also a good way of talking to your child about your pregnancy. Looking at pictures of them when they were small can be an introduction to the whole subject of babies and a way of preparing them for the arrival of a sibling.

My daughter also joined in with my yoga exercises. I cannot say that her participation helped me to relax a great deal, but practice did help to make me more supple and we both enjoyed ourselves. Even now she occasionally lies down on the floor with her legs against the wall and announces that she is doing her 'yoghurt'.

Coping with sleeping problems

Coping with an older child during the daylight hours can be tough during a working pregnancy, but with a little imagination and planning it can be made more enjoyable. Coping at night, when you desperately need your sleep in order to face another working day, is another matter.

Sleeping problems with toddlers are only too common. Lack of sleep is not a problem for children; it is generally accepted that they will sleep for as long as they need to. But it is when their sleeping pattern does not coincide with your sleep needs that *your* problems really start.

Child-care expert Penelope Leach says that about 20 per cent of children up to the age of two wake one or more times almost every night *and wake their parents*. In fact, all humans have moments during the night when they surface from deeper periods of sleep. Most times we only half wake up, turn over and settle down again. But some children wake up properly and find it hard to drift back to sleep.

It can be infuriating to haul yourself out of bed only to discover there is absolutely nothing wrong with a child, apart from the fact that he or she wants company in the wee small hours. And I speak from personal experience.

Even if you have managed to put up with broken nights before a second pregnancy, the situation can become intolerable once you are expecting another baby and have to get up and go to work the next morning. At least non-working mothers might have a chance to catch up with some sleep if their first child still has a day-time nap.

An awful lot of parents solve the problem by taking the child to bed with them, because then at least they are not up and down half the night. While this can be all right as a short-term solution, it may not be so good in the long term. You have to consider whether you are going to be able to get your child used to sleeping alone again. And the method does not always work anyway.

I used to use this as a final resort with my daughter and it worked well. She would settle down with no trouble at all, and could usually be moved, still sleeping, back to her own bed. Taking her in with me for a cuddle was much better than getting in and out of bed to see to her every fifteen minutes or so.

When I tried the same technique with my son, however, it was a different story. He simply treats the whole thing as a game and proceeds to wake us all up fully by playing peep-bo under the covers.

You may also have to train yourself not to leap out of bed at the first whimper. It is quite possible that your child will have a bit of a moan and then go back to sleep, but if you rush in at the first sound, you will almost certainly wake him up properly.

Can you find a reason?
Noise can also bring a half-awake child to full consciousness. If your child sleeps in the front of the house, where he is more likely to hear car doors slamming or a motorbike zooming past at midnight, it might be worth rearranging the bedrooms if you can, even if it means you sleeping in his smaller room while he has the 'master' bedroom at the back.

On the other hand, total quiet and dark may worry him. Lots of parents find that some kind of night lamp does the trick. Even putting a ticking clock in the room has worked for some.

If a child gets cold in the early hours because he has kicked off all his blankets, you could try putting an all-in-one-sleep suit over his pyjamas instead.

If your child does not already take his favourite soft toy to bed it might be worth fostering the habit. Then, if he wakes in the night, Teddy might be comfort enough without needing to yell for

Mummy. If your child already takes a cuddly to bed, make sure you fish it out from under the bedclothes so that it is easy for him to find, before you yourself go to bed.

Breaking the pattern
The trouble is that children easily fall into patterns of behaviour and before you know where you are, you are locked into a situation which repeats itself over and over again. If a child has got used to waking in the night it may be difficult to change his ways. You may have to harden your heart.

I am not suggesting that you should ignore a child who wakes up and cries for you in the night. But when you go to him you should provide as little stimulation as possible. Don't chat. Limit your conversation to finding out what the matter is, make sure that the child is not too hot, too cold, too wet, too thirsty. Offer plain water rather than juice. Don't put the main light on, and if possible don't lift the child out of his bed or cot. Be reassuring but firm. It is night-time and everybody, including Mummy, is in bed and going to sleep. Then close the bedroom door – and your ears.

If you can bear to be persistent, this policy may pay off. Your child will eventually get the message that Mummy will come if something is wrong, but that night-time is a time for sleeping rather than for socializing. But you may have to get to desperation pitch before you can bring yourself to try it.

One woman said: 'I'd put up with all the broken nights, thinking all the time that it was just a stage. First I used to say she woke because she was hungry, so I breastfed her. Then I put it down to teeth. Then I stopped trying to think of reasons and just got into the routine of having to get up two or three times a night to give her a cuddle and lull her back to sleep. I managed to cope at work, despite the fact that I could have done with more sleep myself, until I got pregnant. By this time my daughter was two and a bit, as bright as a button and perfectly able to tell me if something was wrong and understand what I was saying to her.

'At this point I was so desperate for a good night's sleep that I stopped worrying about my daughter and started getting angry. I was determined to change things. So I started a policy of going in once to check that everything was all right and to reassure her. Then I told her that I was going back to sleep and that she should lie down, be quiet and try to go to sleep too. Then I shut the door and let her yell.

'The first few nights were hell. She yelled for ages and I got even less sleep than ever. But on the fifth night she only yelled for five minutes and the night after that it was just a token protest. And the night after that she didn't wake me up at all. Since then, she only occasionally wakes and calls for me, but I think that's when she's had a bad dream. I don't mind that. What I did mind was the situation that we'd got into, where everything was focussed on her and what she needed, and not on what I needed too.'

Leaving a child to cry is worth trying, at least for a week, if your nerves can stand it. But whatever tack you take try one thing at a time and give each possible solution a chance to work.

In this chapter I have only briefly outlined some of the most common approaches used by parents desperate to get an uninterrupted night's sleep. If none of these seem to work, don't give up. So many parents face this problem that whole books have been written on the subject. One of these is listed on page 183, but find out what else your library or local bookshop have to offer.

If you can summon up the energy to tackle the problem properly now, you will be doing yourself a favour; not just for the remainder of the pregnancy, but also for the future when you will have another baby waking up in the night.

10
Back to work – or not?

At some point during your pregnancy you are going to have to think about life after the baby and whether you will want to go back to work. If you want to return to your present job, you will have to decide three weeks before you begin your maternity leave, because this is when you must inform your employer in writing for the first time (see chapter 2).

It is not easy trying to look into a crystal ball to see what the future holds: my advice would be to keep all your options open. You may find yourself under all kinds of conflicting pressures from those around you. Perhaps your boss is not entirely happy about holding a job open for you. In-laws or acquaintances may tell you that children need their mothers at home. Work-mates may warn you that if you jump off the career ladder now you will never get back on, and so on and so on.

Listen to them by all means, and listen, in particular, to your partner. Whatever you decide will be much harder to handle if it is entirely against his wishes. A working mother needs all the support she can get at home, and it is no fun for the stay-at-home mother to be sniped at by a husband who thinks she is leading the life of Reilly and ought to be doing a real day's work and bringing in some extra money.

How do you really feel?
Listen to your own instincts, too, and be prepared for the possibility that those feelings may change after you have had the baby. You may be one of the lucky women whose ideas on the subject of being a working mother are so clear-cut that your decision does not involve any heart-searching.

A sales assistant aged twenty-three said: 'I would love to have got a job after the baby was born, but I feel that the first couple of years or so are very important to a child, so I wouldn't have left her with anyone.

'I want to spend the time with my daughter that my Mum did with me. She taught me to read and do sums before I started school and those first years with her will never be forgotten. Providing we do not have another child, I will go out to work in two or three years.'

A woman of thirty-two, who worked as a care assistant in a home for the elderly, had been trying for a baby for so long that after her daughter was born she did not want to miss any of her babyhood. 'I had been trying to get pregnant for eight years, and after many tests, hormone treatments and consultations I was told I was infertile.

'The joy and fulfilment I feel caring for our daughter is enough for me. Although financially I could do with some extra money. I'm happily broke.'

On the other hand, there are many women who never dream of giving up work, but decide from the outset that they are going to have a baby and keep their job. A reasearcher said: 'It never occurred to me that the two things were mutually exclusive. My own mother worked as a teacher when we were all young and I don't think it did us any harm. I enjoyed the six months I spent at home looking after my son, but I was very pleased to get back to work and have something other than feeds and nappies to occupy my mind. I got on very well with the childminder and, more importantly, so did the baby. I look after him for as many of his waking hours as she does, so I certainly don't think I'm missing out on motherhood.

'In fact, I probably do it better and enjoy it more, simply because I don't have to do it all the time.'

Some facts and figures

Most women do not return to their jobs after maternity leave. A report published by Incomes Data Services in 1985 says: 'There are exceptions; in certain jobs, or more accurately certain professions, many women do return to their former posts. But they are in a minority.'

According to the General Household Survey of 1983, just under 5 per cent of all women with a child under five had a full-time job. By no means all of these would have returned to work immediately after taking maternity leave.

The most detailed study on maternity leave so far is the one that was carried out by the Policy Studies Institute for the Department of Employment in 1979. It found that only half of the women who worked during pregnancy qualified for maternity pay and reinstatement. But even this does not explain why relatively few women go back to work straightaway after having a baby.

Although one in two women had the right to go back, only one in ten did so, and only a third of these went back to the same job, working the same hours. Most of the women went back to work part-time.

But there are signs that the pattern may be changing. The Alfred Marks survey of office staff, for instance, shows that 15.5 per cent returned to work in 1983, but 31 per cent did so in 1985. And the IDS report quotes the Burton Group as saying: 'I think it would be fair to say that the trend towards women returning to work after maternity leave is growing – particularly at our Head Office site (London).'

Of the women who took part in my survey (admittedly a self-selected sample), the vast majority had babies born in 1984 or

1985. Of these, 40 per cent said they had full-time jobs, 14 per cent said they were intending to go back to work and a further 14 per cent were working part-time.

Altogether, then, around two-thirds were already back at work or intending to return, while about a third had given up work or were not intending to go back.

Feelings of guilt
When you are weighing up the pros and cons of going back to work, you will have to take all kinds of factors into account. One of these is the thorny old question of whether you will be 'a better mother' if you stay at home.

A qualified teacher, who has two children aged five and three, told me how she wrestles with the problem. 'I love working, but feel guilty at leaving the children and if I don't work I feel guilty because I could be adding to the family coffers and furthering my career for later on. I have sometimes worked since the children were born, using childminders. But now my youngest has reached the age where he needs to do things like go swimming, join playgroups, and so on. I cannot expect a childminder to do these things.

'So now I am in a "Catch 22" situation. Do I go back to work, therefore making me a "better person" (as my husband would like me to), but deserting my son? Or do I stay at home, champing at the bit, and be a "good mother"?'

A friend of mine, another journalist, found her own way of solving the dilemma. She says: 'When I had young children and went off to work I tended to feel guilty. This was mainly because I enjoyed my work so much more than looking after little children. But I stopped feeling guilty the minute I read a book by an Americal psychologist which underlines exactly how pointless guilt is.

'Guilt is caused by anxiety about past actions which can never, whatever the consequences, be altered. Guilt is debilitating and ageing, and is liable to affect the working mother with young children more than any other section of society. Once you make up your mind to banish guilt from your life, as I did, the rest becomes comparatively easy.

'I believe that the difficulties of combining a job with bringing up a family have been greatly over-exaggerated, and nowadays any woman who wants to can perfectly well do both.'

Fighting words. But for those of us who are not convinced that it is quite so easy to banish guilt, it is worth taking a look at some of the evidence on the effect a mother's employment may have on her children.

How will the children fare?

First of all, let us examine the idea that a child needs the constant loving attention of its *mother* if it is to grow into a balanced adult. It is interesting to note that the 'babies need their mothers' theory (with the underlying implication that they need their mothers *all the time*) is a notion that has gained impetus only in this century.

As child-care expert Penelope Leach says: 'You might like to bear in mind the fact that demands for mothers to care for their babies *alone and constantly* are a recent phenomenon. In our own society in the past, and in many societies today, a baby's care was always shared between mothers, elder sisters, grandmothers and so forth.'

Penelope Leach suggests that babies do need consistent and continuous care that allows them to build up relationships and develop as social beings, but she also points out that this need not be provided by one person – the mother – alone.

Or, as sociologist Ann Oakley puts it: 'There is no evidence that adult mental health is dependent on childhood care by one's biological mother, or by any mother: infants have a capacity for surviving, unharmed, those discontinuities in relationships that are, in fact, a normal part of life.'

In other words, it probably makes little difference whether you look after your baby yourself all day, or whether you share his care with others. What matters is the way in which you spend the time you have with your child, and the way others spend time with him.

How your baby is cared for

Obviously it is not going to help your baby develop if he is left with a childminder who feeds him, changes him and generally cares for his physical needs, but spends little time talking to him or playing with him. On the other hand, having an extra loving adult in his life can be a positive bonus.

Penelope Leach herself has reservations about leaving a baby at a day nursery, however well-equipped it is, or however well qualified the staff are. She says: 'In a group he may always be cared for by the same people, but, because he must compete with too many other babies, he may simply not get as much attention as he can use.'

However, in their discussion book *Working Women,* the TUC make the point that there is evidence to show that young children *benefit* from going to a nursery. A recent study showed that:

> Children of eighteen months in day-care got on better with other children and their learning was more advanced.
> When re-tested at four and a half, the children who had been in day-care were more advanced at speaking
> Children who had been in day-care were just as attached to their mothers.

One of the difficulties in making judgments about what effect a mother's job has on her baby is that there has been very little proper research into the subject. But there has been quite a lot of work on the effects of maternal employment on older children.

Some conclusions for working mothers

In general, the picture for working mothers is reassuring:
1. There is no conclusive evidence to suggest that children whose mothers work do better or worse at school than those whose mothers do not
2. There is no evidence to support the idea that just because a mother works, her children will lack supervision or turn into juvenile delinquents
3. There does seem to be a difference between boys and girls. Girls whose mothers work are likely to be more independent, higher achievers and have a more positive view of what women can do, than those whose mothers do not work. However, this does not apply to boys.

Another factor to bear in mind is the knock-on effect: if working makes you happier, the chances are you will enjoy the time you do spend with your children. The more positive and self-confident you are as a person, the more self-confident and positive you will be as a mother.

One study has shown that mothers who did not have either full or part-time jobs outside the home were more likely to suffer from depression than those who did. It must surely be better to have a mother who works but isn't depressed, than one who doesn't and is?

Even Penelope Leach makes the point that if a mother is not happy, for whatever reason, then she cannot make her baby happy either: 'From the infant's point of view, somebody responsive and sociable is a must... what may deprive him is being alone with a mother who is withdrawn from involvement with him...'

Will you miss the challenge of work?

One of the difficulties in trying to decide whether or not you want to go back to work after the baby is born, especially if it is your first baby, is that you really have no idea what it will be like to be at home with your child. Some women find it completely fulfilling and exciting. Others miss the challenges of work and the contact with other adults.

An accounting officer who left work when she had her baby soon changed her mind. She says: 'I thought I wouldn't want to return, but by the time my daughter was nine months old I couldn't bear having nothing to do. Even so, it was very hard to leave my daughter and to find the right person to take care of her while I was at work. I still think it was the right decision. My daughter hasn't suffered at all and I'm much happier all round.'

A journalist said: 'I don't think I have ever looked forward to anything quite so much as my first day back at work after maternity leave, although when I went off to have the baby I was worried that twenty-nine weeks wouldn't be long enough. My friends thought I was crazy to go back and even my husband was convinced that I would regret it.

'But I blossomed – and so did the baby. I admit that we'd had a tough few months. We ended up moving house just after the baby was born and then spent the first few months being rewired, replumbed and redecorated. The weather didn't help. It was winter and when it wasn't snowing it was raining. It's all very well to talk of bonding – we had little choice, the baby and I. It was like being in prison. I missed my friends from work, the laughs, the gossip. There were days when I spoke to no one but the baby until my husband came home.

'Even when the better weather came, the effort involved in getting out with all the paraphernalia one small person seems to need, made it hardly worth the effort. No wonder that the prospect of getting back to work beckoned like the light at the end of a long tunnel.

'I'm sure that makes me sound heartless, but I'm not. I love my daughter dearly. But I felt it would be better for both of us if I could be me again, not just me, a mother. And I am sure I was right.'

Keeping your options open
The fact that it is so difficult to predict your reactions to full-time motherhood is the most important reason for keeping your option to return open. It is no disaster to change your mind and decide not to go back after all, but it could be terrible to realize you have made a mistake after your old job has been given to someone else on a permanent basis.

Some women do, in fact, realize once they have returned to work that things are not working out as they hoped. A nurse said: 'I went back part-time after the baby was born, but I only worked for three months. I simply found it too difficult and too tiring to cope with.'

And a doctor said: 'I'd always seen myself as a career woman. But after the baby was born my priorities seemed to change. I did go back to work after maternity leave, but I just wasn't interested in what I call the politics of work. I still enjoyed certain aspects, the caring side, if you like. But I realized that the commitment wasn't there any more.

'I resented the fact that someone else was giving my baby a bath, teaching her how to climb the stairs, playing silly games with her. So I decided to leave and put my career on hold. I intend to go back, but not yet. I want to enjoy my baby while I can.'

If you decide to leave your options open when you actually go off on maternity leave, remember that you do not have to be hurried into making a final decision after this. Your employer has the right to ask you for a written confirmation seven weeks after the date of your confinement that you intend to return. Once, again, unless you are obsolutely sure that full-time motherhood is for you, keep your options open by saying that you do. After all, you are entitled to twenty-nine weeks, providing that you meet the requirements to qualify for leave in the first place. You have to give your employer at least three weeks' written notice of the day on which you want to start work again. If you were to take the maximum leave, your baby will be six months old at this point, and the difference between a seven-week-old baby and a six-month-old is enormous. More to the point, your feelings about whether you want to be a full-time mother may have changed too.

How employers feel

The PSI study on maternity leave which I mentioned earlier found that about 9 per cent of the firms involved complained about the inconvenience of keeping jobs open or finding replacements for women on maternity leave. A few said that it created difficulties if they could not be certain that women who said they were going to return would actually do so. And a few complained about women not coming back, although they had given notice that they would.

Overall, however, the study said that reinstatement was 'occasionally an irritant for some but very rarely generated substantial problems.'

Some women take the view that it is wrong to hang on to your right to return unless you are really committed to doing so. They argue that women who say they are going to do one thing and then do another give all women a bad reputation. My own view is that women have pretty poor maternity rights in this country, and that we should make the best use of the rights we do have and turn them to our advantage when possible. It is also worth bearing in mind that the number of women taking maternity leave is tiny compared with general staff turnover and the problems this may cause for employers.

In addition, most companies make temporary appointments to cover for women on maternity leave and presumably, if you do decide at the last moment not to go back to work, the temporary cover can be extended or turned into a permanent position. In any case, many women are in jobs where they can give a month's notice: even if you decide at twenty-six weeks after the birth that you are not going to go back, you have only cut the usual notice period by a week.

If you need the money

Career advancement and self-fulfilment are two reasons for returning to work which give a woman a choice. She can decide how she feels when the time comes. But some women do not have this choice. They have to work during pregnancy and afterwards because they need the money.

A music teacher said: 'I returned to work twelve weeks after the baby was born for financial reasons. I regret this as I feel I missed a lot of her early days.'

To anyone who has to go back to work, despite all her inclinations, because she needs the money, I can only say this: don't spend your emotional energy in sadness, guilt or resentment. Try to accept things the way they are and make the most of the time you do have with your child.

After all, a baby won't care if you don't iron the cot sheets, but he will notice if you don't have time to play pat-a-cake. Your toddler won't care if you don't dust the living room, but he will mind if you haven't got time to read him a bedtime story.

Some women go back to work because their wages make all the difference between mere survival and having a halfway decent life. For others the situation is not so critical, but they prefer to have some money they can call their own.

A building society cashier said: 'I did give up my job when I was pregnant because we had worked out that we could manage on one salary and, anyway, I wanted to be at home with the baby.

'I didn't find being at home boring – I really enjoyed the time I spent with the baby and I made some new friends who had had babies at the same time as me.

'What I missed most was having some money to call my own. We had to watch what we spent and although I didn't mind spending money on things for the baby, I felt incredibly guilty about buying myself a magazine or a new jumper. We'd always had a joint bank account, and when I was working I didn't mind paying for something like my husband's birthday present out of it, because I had put money in.

'But I hated using his money to buy him a gift. My husband used to say I was being silly, that it was our money no matter who earned it. But it mattered to me.'

Part-time work

Of course, even if you decide not to take up your option of reinstatement, because you do not want to go back to the same job, working the same hours, when the baby is still only a few months old, that does not mean you have to give up the idea of working altogether.

It might be worth exploring the possibility of going back part-time. Employers these days *are* concerned about losing capable trained staff and some make special efforts to encourage women to return to work after having babies, both by extending the statutory length of paid or unpaid maternity leave, and/or by enabling women to start back on a part-time basis.

In the Civil Service, for instance, a programme of action on equality for women has been agreed, which includes 'encouragement to Departments to ensure that the provisions for maternity leave, part-time work and special leave (such as time off if children are ill) are brought to the attention of staff as necessary'.

The maximum period of maternity leave was extended to fifty-two weeks and although the expansion of part-time working was left to the discretion of individual departments, some of them have now provided many more opportunities for women to go back to work on this basis.

A lot of women work part-time in the National Health Service, and although there is no absolute right for a woman who previously worked full-time to return part-time, this can be negotiated with the employing regional health authority and 'consent will not be unreasonably refused'.

Marks and Spencer also acknowledge the fact that some women may wish to return on a part-time basis. 'Whilst this is not an entitlement, if a vacancy exists at the planned time of return and the woman is suitable for the vacancy, she may return part-time.'

Unfortunately, most women who want a part-time job after their baby is born will have to look for a new job altogether. And, in general, part-time work for women is poorly paid and under-utilizes the skills they already have. One of the women in my survey, for example, was a skilled factory worker who ended up working part-time in a local restaurant.

But although this kind of part-time work may not be very satisfying in career terms, and it may not pay very well, it does at least provide some kind of break from the home and contact with other adults. Another attraction is that you may be able to find a part-time job very near your home. Obviously, the less time you spend travelling, the more time you can spend with your baby, and the less you will have to pay someone else to look after him.

Job-sharing

Another possibility, and one that is becoming slightly more common, is that of job-sharing. It has been very successful in America but is still in its infancy in Britain. Basically, two part-time workers share one full-time job between them. Each worker has the advantage of a shorter working week, yet both still get security of tenure, holiday pay, and so on – benefits which are not always available for ordinary part-time workers.

So far very few private companies have introduced the idea and if you are interested you may have to persuade your bosses that the system could work. You would have to find your other 'half', work out the hours you would each work, how you would liase, what sort of responsibility each would take, and so on.

The Equal Opportunities Commission publishes a booklet on job-sharing and you can contact a charity called New Ways to Work for help and advice. They also run a register of people living in the Greater London area, to match would-be job-sharers.

Is it cost-effective to work?

If you are considering returning to work in some capacity in the relatively near future, it is important to do your sums. How much is it going to cost to pay someone else to carry out the child-care you would have done for nothing? How much will you spend on getting to and from work? How much extra would you be spending on clothes for work – you won't be able to hide a pair of laddered tights under your jeans as you could at home. How much will go on extras such as cups of coffee, sandwiches, office leaving presents? Will you be spending more on convenience foods to eat at home if you don't have time to cook?

On top of this you have to weigh up all the things you can't put a price on: your independence, keeping a career on target, the confidence you get from doing a job, the stimulation you get from being with colleagues. Against all this is the deep attachment you feel for your baby, and the joy you get from being a mother.

Finding someone to look after your child
If you decide to go back to work, whether full or part-time, after maternity leave or at some later stage, your biggest headache will be finding someone to look after your child. As one woman put it: 'Working through pregnancy was easy – it was making all the arrangements to work afterwards that was the problem!'

Day nurseries and creches
You may like the idea of putting your child in a creche or nursery, but you will be lucky to find one. There just are not enough places to go round and most, whether state or privately run, do not take children under the age of two. Even if you are offered a place, the travelling involved or the hours it is open may not suit your circumstances.

A midwife said: 'As a single parent I didn't have much choice about going back to work, but I also feel I need to work for my own sake. To be sitting around at home all day isn't my idea of fun.

'When my son was a year old I was offered a nursery place five miles in the opposite direction from the hospital where I work. It didn't open until 7.30 a.m. and as I sometimes have to start work at 7.45 a.m. it was out of the question. Also, my shift pattern occasionally means I have to work until around 9 p.m.

'Luckily I have been able to find a childminder who will look after my son until 9.30 p.m. if necessary, but very few will do this.'

If you are looking for a day nursery, contact your local Social Services department for information. If there is not a nursery locally, you may be tempted to try and get your employer to set one up, particularly if you work for a large company. You would probably be wasting your time, however. These things can take years to organize and if a scheme ever did get off the ground your children would probably by then be too old to qualify. In any case, rightly or wrongly, most employers are not keen on work-place nurseries, partly because they say they are expensive for employees compared with other forms of child-care but also, they claim, because parents do not want to drag their children into city centres and other busy areas.

On the other hand, mothers do feel there should be more state provision. Three years ago I was involved in a survey of working mothers carried out by the *Daily Express*. Although only 2 per cent of those who took part actually used state nurseries or creches, 70 per cent felt there should be more provision of this kind.

Because there were so few nurseries, the majority of women had to have makeshift arrangements with family and friends. 'I work part-time,' said one office worker, 'but I couldn't do it if my mother didn't have the children. I feel it's crazy that at thirty-four still have to rely on her. I can't be independent.'

Childminders

Quite a high proportion of these women – about one in five – relied on childminders, rather than friends or relations. Usually they dropped their child off in the morning at the childminder's house, and collected him on the way home from work. Occasionally, the childminder came to the mother's house.

You can advertise in the local paper for a childminder or contact your local Social Services department for a list of registered childminders. They may also be able to tell you which ones have vacancies and would consider taking a child the age of yours.

A registered childminder will have been vetted by the Social Services, and her house checked for space, cleanliness and safety. She may have had no formal training (although she will often be a mother herself) but she might have been on a special course. You should also do some checking yourself. When you visit her home, see what kind of toys she provides and what state they are in. Ask what kind of activities she will offer your baby during the day. Will she take him out to the shops or the park, let him play in the garden, and so on?

If you are considering this option, you should get hold of the leaflet *I need a childminder* from the National Childminding Association and, if you decide to go ahead, make sure that you introduce your baby to the childminder well before you go back to work, so that they have time to get to know each other.

A live-in nanny or mother's help

Relatively few mothers can afford a live-in nanny or mother's help, but if you can, it may be the best solution. Your child will have the continuity of being cared for in his own home and you will not have to worry so much if you cannot get back from work dead on time.

On the other hand, you will have to get used to having a stranger in the house. She may end up being a friend, but equally she could cause extra problems.

Try to decide in advance what you want. Some nannies have been formally trained. Others learned the job as they went along. A qualified National Nursery Examining Board and experienced nanny will be the most expensive type. A newly qualified NNEB may ask a lower salary than an untrained but experienced nanny, but she will be applying theory rather than practice to the job. Only you can decide what you can afford and whether you want to go for training, experience or a mixture of the two.

There are agencies who specialize in supplying domestic staff like nannies and mother's helps, but their fees are usually fairly hefty. The time-honoured way is to advertise in *The Lady,* but the way you word the advertisement is important. If you want someone who is an NNEB, you must say so, or you will be inundated with calls from girls who just fancy the idea of looking after a baby rather than working in an office, or from visiting Australians looking for a job that will finance the next leg of their travels.

The wage you will have to pay depends on the hours you expect a girl to work and the kind of accommodation and other perks (use of a car, own television and so on) that you can offer. A rather sneaky way of finding out what the going rates are is to get hold of a copy of *The Lady* and ring some of the advertisers as if to apply for a few jobs. Or you can simply come clean and ask other mothers who are advertising what they are prepared to pay.

If you decide to have a live-in help, avoid unnecessary problems cropping up later by working out the house rules before you offer someone a job and making sure that these are acceptable to her. Possible flashpoints include time off, babysitting, male visitors, sick leave, cooking and bathroom arrangements, and, not least, how you want your child to be brought up. If you are hot on table manners, for instance, it is no good having a girl who sees meal times as a chance for free expression. If you think a child should never, ever be smacked, don't pick someone who believes in the odd wallop. And always check references.

Retraining for work
Given the difficulties of finding the right kind of child-care at a price they can afford, it is not surprising that even women who would like to return to work do not always do so. But if that applies to you, it does not mean you have to stay at home for ever.

There are an increasing number of courses for women who want to go back to work after a 'baby break'. Check your local library or further education college for further details when the time comes. Consider the possibilities of using the time at home to develop new skills, and don't under-estimate the homemaking talents you will have the chance to improve. In her book *The Working Woman's Guide* (Thorsons, 1985), Liz Hodgkinson writes:

> The years spent childminding and homemaking will have taught you valuable lessons about yourself, that may not have been apparent when you were a working girl.
> 'You have very probably discovered skills you never knew you had, such as gardening, cooking, dressmaking or balancing budgets. All of these can eventually be turned to commercial advantage, given the will and determination.'

In many ways, having a baby is a turning point in a woman's life. Motherhood can be so many different things to different women. But once you have a baby one thing is sure; life will never be the same again.

In the early months after the birth of your child you should give yourself time to adjust, to learn what being a mother means to you without making any irrevocable decisions about your long-term future as a working woman. By all means think about that future, but also give yourself time to enjoy your baby as much as you have, I hope, enjoyed working through your pregnancy.

Useful books and information

Book list
Pregnancy and Childbirth, Sheila Kitzinger (Michael Joseph, 1980).
The Pregnancy Survival Manual, Professor Geoffrey Chamberlain, (Macdonald, 1984).
The Complete Handbook of Pregnancy, consultant editor, Wendy Rose-Neil (Sphere, 1984).
Pregnancy, Gordon Bourne (Pan, 1984).
Pregnant Women at Work, edited by Professor Geoffrey Chamberlain (Royal Society of Medicine/Macmillan, 1984). This book is based on papers given at the Anglo-American conference held at the Royal Society of Medicine in London in 1983. Speakers at the conference were invited to contribute a chapter on the aspect of work and pregnancy in which he or she was an expert. Much of the research which I referred to in chapter 1 is contained in this book.
Active Birth, Janet Balaskas (Unwin Paperbacks, 1983).
Easy Pregnancy with Yoga, Stella Weller (Thorsons, 1979).
Inner Beauty, Inner Light, F. Leboyer (Collins, 1979).
Exercises for Childbirth, Barbara Dale and Johanna Roeber (Century, 1982).
The Jane Fonda Workout Book for Pregnancy, Birth and Recovery, Femmy Delyser (Allen Lane, 1983). You can also buy a video based on this book.
The Childbirth Book, Christine Beels (Mayflower, 1980).
Marriage, Maureen Green (Fontana, 1983).
Babyhood, Penelope Leach (Pelican, 1983). This book has a chapter on sleep and its problems.
Sleepless Children: a Handbook for Parents, Dr David Haslam (Piatkus, 1984).

Solve Your Child's Sleep Problems, Dr Richard Ferber (Dorling Kindersley, 1985).
The Working Woman's Guide, Liz Hodgkinson (Thorsons, 1985). Has useful chapters on working mothers, going back to work and retraining.
The Parents' A to Z, Penelope Leach (Penguin, 1985). Has a chapter on working mothers.

Books and leaflets about your rights during pregnancy
Babies and benefits, Department of Health and Social Security.
Employment rights of the expectant mother, Department of Employment (available from Jobcentres and advice centres).
Single and pregnant, a guide to benefits for single mothers, National Council for One Parent Families, 255 Kentish Town Road, London NW5 2LX. Tel: 01-267 1361.
Parenthood in the balance and how to prepare your own case for an industrial tribunal, The Equal Opportunities Commission, Overseas House, Quay Street, Manchester M3 3HN. Tel: 061-833 9244.
Pregnancy Book, The Health Education Council, 78 New Oxford Street, London WC1A 1AH. Tel: 01-637 1881 (also available from your ante-natal clinic). This book has a clear section on rights and benefits.
Know your rights series, The Maternity Alliance, 56-61 Camden High Street, London NW1 7JL. Tel: 01-388 6337. This is a campaigning organization which can give advice and information. They also publish a useful booklet, *Getting fit for pregnancy.*
Maternity Rights Handbook, Ruth Evans and Lyn Durward (Penguin, 1984). (compiled by the Maternity Alliance).

Useful addresses

The National Childbirth Trust, 9 Queensborough Terrace, London W2 3TB. Tel: 01-221 3833

Foresight, The Old Vicarage, Church Lane, Witley, Godalming, Surrey GU8 5PN. Tel: Wormley (042879) 4500

The British Homoeopathic Association, 27A Devonshire Street, London W1N 1RJ. Tel: 01-935 2163. They have a booklet called *Homoeopathy for mother and infant* by Douglas Borland.

Health Education Council, 78 New Oxford street, London WC1A 1AH. Tel: 01-637 1881. They publish a leaflet called *So you want to stop smoking.*

West London Birth Centre, 7 Waldemar Avenue, Ealing, London W13 (for addresses and information about local birth centres; enclose a stamped, addressed envelope).

The National Childminding Association, 204 High Street, Bromley, Kent BR1 1PP. Tel: 01-464 6164.

New Ways to Work, 347A Upper Street, London N1. Tel: 01-226 4026

Index

abdominal muscles, 76
abnormalities, 22
adult education centres, 97
alcohol, 57, 60
   foetal alcohol syndrome, 57
Alfred Marks survey, 169
alternative work, 36
ante-natal
   appointments, 32, 131
   classes, 118, 133-148, 153-154
   clinic, 37, 96
aromatherapy, 69, 73
Ashley, Laura, 63, 72
Association of Scientific, Technical and Managerial Staffs, 21

backache, 77, 79, 87, 95, 142
   chronic, 81
   sacro-iliac pain, 92
Beels, Christine, 136
Belgium, pregnancy entitlements in, 40
bending and lifting, 79
birth, 114, 134-137, 141, 145, 147, 152-153, 182
   centre, 140, 147
   high-tech, 135
   natural, 135, 136
birthweight, 16
   low, 17, 55, 57
bladder, 52, 77
bleeding, 46, 55
blood
   analysis, 24
   pressure, 17, 24, 47, 56, 102, 115, 158
Blooming Marvellous, 62, 72
body language, 113
bottle feeding, 138
breaking the news at work, 45
breastfeeding, 138, 145, 157, 165
breathing, 83, 96, 141, 142, 152, *see also* Relaxation techniques
British Medical Journal, 20
British Perinatal Mortality Survey, 1958, 17
Bumpsadaisy, 64

Caesarian section, 31, 140-142
career, pregnancy's effect on, 105-106, 176
cervix, 136
cervical stitch, 81
Chamberlain, Professor Geoffrey, 15, 18, 29, 75
chemicals, 19
   dangerous substances, 20
Childbirth Book, The, 136
child-care, 139, 161, 169, 170, 171, 172, 179-181
   agencies, 181
   fees, 181
chiropody, 69
chloasma, 68
Citizen's Advice Bureau, 36, 37
clothes, 62-73, 152·
   Blooming Marvellous, 62
   borrowing, 64
   Bumpsadaisy, 64
   choosing, 62
   hiring, 64
   Laura Ashley, 63
   materials, 65
   Mothercare, 62, 63
   shoes, 66
   summer, 65
   underwear, 66-67
   Vogue patterns, 63
   winter, 65, 66
contraception, 24
   alternative methods, 24
contractions, 141, 142
complications, 22, 81
coping
   at work, 49
   with a second child, 153, 161, 163
cramp, 77, 95

dental treatment, 38, 69
Department of Employment Survey, 1980, 39
   study by Policy Studies Institute, 1979, 169, 175
Department of Health and Social Security, 39

depression, 173
diet, 23, 50, 58-59, 68
   additives, 23
   advice on, 69
   canteen food, 59
   fruit, 24, 58
   highly processed foods, 23
   metal contamination, 24
   vegetables, 24
   unrefined foods, 24
dismissal, 32, 44, 47
   fair, 32
   unfair, 36
drugs, 135-137, 142, 146, 153, *see also* entries under brand names
dysphoria, 71

Employment
   Appeal Tribunal, 44
   Protection Act, 44
enema, 142, 147
Entonox, 146
epidural, 136, 144, 146, 152
episiotomy, 142, 146, 147
Equal Opportunities Commission, 39, 41, 44
equipment, 139
Ethiopian women, 18
exercise, 24, 74-97, 140, 147
   for baby in posterior position, 80
   for backache, 79, 87, 92, 93-94
   for easing constipation, 93
   for heartburn, 85, 88
   for improving circulation, 85, 88, 93
   for loosening hips, 85
   for loosening shoulders, 87
   for opening chest, 85
   for pelvic floor, 85, 93
   for relaxing muscles, 87
   for strengthening lower back, 88
   for thigh muscles, 85, 91
   for varicose veins, 89-91
   in your own home, 76
   pain, 75
   pelvic circling, 80
   pelvic rocking, 80
   stiffness, 82
   swimming, 75
   vigorous/dangerous, 75
   yoga, 76-77
eyes, 67

fainting, 52
fatigue, 19, 22, 47, 53, 59, 77, 80, 119, 129, 156, 158-159
Family Practitioner Committee, 38
flexible hours (Flexitime), 25, 53, 103

foetal
   alcohol syndrome, 57
   monitor, 137, 141, 142, 146
forceps, 137
Foresight, 24
France, pregnancy entitlements in, 40
French national birth survey, 1972, 17
   study, 1977 and 1978, 19
full-time work, 33, 34, 38, 43, 74, 117, 119, 126, 157, 169, 170, 173

General Household Survey, 1983, 169
German measles (rubella), 24
Government, the, 42
GP, 24, 37, 38, 96, 135, 144, 147
Green, Maureen, 156
guilt, 56, 170, 176

haemorrhage, 55
haemorrhoids, 88, 91
hair, 68-69
   tints, 68
   perms, 68
headaches, 78
health
   centre, 140, 147
   visitor, 24, 37, 144, 147
heartburn, 85, 88
Hodgkinson, Liz, 182
home helps, 118, 126, 161
homoeopathic doctors/pharmacists, 51
hormones, 47, 48, 50, 52, 68, 70
hospital, 140, 142, 144, 145, 146-147
household chores, 117-127, 160-161
   cooking, 122
   division of labour, 126, 127, 155
   equipment, 121-122
   organization of, 120-121
   shopping, 124-126
   washing, 123
Hytton, Dr Frank, 18

Incomes Data Services report, 1985, 42, 169
income tax, 34
industrial tribunal, 32, 37, 44, 133
Italy, pregnancy entitlements in, 40
Kitzinger, Sheila, 129, 134, 150

labour, 55, 128, 134-137, 140, 142, 145, 146, 147, 152.
   acceleration of, 142
   induction of, 142
law
   centre, 36, 37
   changes in the, 42
Leach, Penelope, 163, 171, 172, 173

INDEX

McKechnie, Sheila, 21, 22
Marks and Spencer, 177
Marriage, 156
maternity
  Alliance, 36, 133
  allowance, 34, 35, 37, 39, 40, 43
  benefits, 26, 31, 37, 38, 40
  grant, 37
  leave, 30, 31, 35, 36, 39, 40, 41, 42, 43, 44, 46, 53, 108-109, 128, 133, 134, 154, 158, 167, 169, 173, 174, 175, 177
  pay, 27, 31, 33, 34, 36, 39, 40, 41, 43, 53, 115, 129, 169
  Pay Fund, 34
  rights, 26, 30, 31, 36, 39, 41, 47, 109-111, 133, 134, 175
  services, 133
medical
  check-ups, 24
  Research Council, Perinatal Medicine Division, 18
midwife, 24, 34, 38, 135, 142, 144, 146, 147, 154
minerals, 24
miscarriage, 28, 46, 49, 55, 75, 81
morning sickness and nausea, 48, 49, 50, 51, 53, 56, 59, 77, 119, 129, 151
money, 28, 35, 60, 177
Mothercare, 62, 63, 71

nasal congestion, 95
National
  Childbirth Trust, 24, 64, 134, 140, 142, 144, 145, 147, 153
  Childminding Association, 180
  Health Service, 51, 177
  insurance contributions, 34, 37
  Nursery Examining Board, 181
nausea, *see* Morning sickness
neonatal death, 55
notice, 34, 35, 36, 175
nutrition, 24, 55, *see also* Diet

Oakley, Ann, 171
Odent, Michel, 134-135
oedema, 102
other mothers, 137-139
overweight, 23

parental leave, 42
part-time work, 33, 34, 38, 41, 43, 157, 159, 170, 173, 174, 177-178, 180
pelvic
  cavity, 77
  exercise for improving circulation in, 93
  exercise for relaxing, 87
  exercise for toning, 85
  floor, 77
perinatal mortality, 118
pethidine, 141, 146, 147
pheromones, 113
physically demanding jobs, 18
physiology, 136, 144
physiotherapist, 144
post-natal recovery, 76
posture, 77
  chairs, 78
  typing, 78
pre-conceptual
  care, 23, 24
  counsellor, 25
pre-eclampsia, 17, 28
Pregnancy and Childbirth, 129, 150
premature
  birth, 22, 55
  labour, 17, 75
prescriptions, 38, 69
pressures at work, 103
private sector, 42
problems
  at work, 100-101
  with company policy, 103
  with maternity leave, 108-109
  with relatives, 131-132
  with your partner, 130-131
professional attitude, 115
public sector, 31, 42

qualifications, 41

redundancy, 36, 41
regulations, 26
reinstatement, 33, 38, 41, 169, 175, 177
relaxation, 82, 153
  techniques, 56, 57, 140, 142, 145, 147
returning to work, 35, 36, 41, 43, 44, 129, 167-182
  career, 176
  'Catch 22' situation, 170
  child-care, 171-172, 178, 181
  effects on children, 171, 172-173
  money, 176
  not returning, 173, 174
rest at work, 54
retraining for work, 182
risks
  anaesthetic, 21
  health, 25
  miscarriage, 21
  possible, 20
  toxic metals, 24
Royal College of Obstetricians and Gynaecologists, 21

rubella (German measles), 24
rupture of the membranes, 142
   premature or artificial, 55, 146

second or third baby, 149-166
   ante-natal classes, 153
   attitudes of other people, 154, 156
   birth, 152-153
   breaking news to first child, 149
   clothes, 152
   fatigue, 158-159
   household chores, 155, 157, 160-161
   maternity leave, 154, 157, 158
   morning sickness, 151
   NCT refresher courses, 153
   sex-life, 156-157
   sleeping problems, 163-166
   support, 155, 158, 160
   travelling, 159, 160
   time with first child, 161-163
   work, 157, 159
sedentary jobs, 76
self-employed, 27, 39
sex, 129-131, 156
   Discrimination Act, 44
   discrimination, 106-108
shave, 142, 147
shoes, 66
single mothers, 38, 132
skin, 68
   chloasma, 68
   cosmetics, 68
   creams, 68
   itchy, 68, 95
sleeplessness, 77, 95
smear, 24
smoking, 25, 60
   danger of, 54
   giving up, 55, 56
   passive, 23, 25
social
   life, 112-113, 127
   security, 37, 40
   Services Department, 179, 180
   Trends Report, The, 1986, 117
stillbirth, 55
stress, 26, 48, 50, 56, 74, 131, 137, 156

support
   at work, 98-100, 101
   after the baby is born, 138-139
   from the relatives, 139
   from your partner, 117, 128, 168
   in second pregnancy, 155, 158, 160
   post-natal, 145
   practical, moral and emotional, 111, 139, 142, 145
syntometrine, 135

teeth, 69-70, *see also* Dental treatment
   plaque, 70
tension, 96
tiredness, *see* fatigue
touch, 114
toxaemia, 17
trade union, 25, 26, 36, 42, 43, 58
   TUC book, *Working Women*, 172
training, 41
travel and travelling, 49, 50, 51, 52, 53, 159, 160, 179
twins, 28

underwear, 66
   bras, 66-67
   knickers, 67
urinary tract infection, 52
urine analysis, 24
uterus, 77

varicose veins, 77
VDUs, 21, 26
vitamins, 24, 51, 68
Vogue patterns, 63

West Germany, pregnancy entitlements in, 39
West London Birth Centre, 96
working
   and Pregnancy symposium, 1983, 15
   environment, 25
   Woman's Guide, 182
workload, 115

X-rays, 21

yoga, 76-77, 80, 81, 140
   Iyengar Yoga Trust, 97

Of further interest...

PREGNANCY AND CHILDBIRTH

A vital guide for the first-time mother-to-be on the changes to expect in her own body, and the kind of assistance and options open to her through the health service. **Nicky Wesson** gives practical advice on all aspects of pregnancy, including ways in which a woman can determine what is happening to her body and her baby without the aid of professionals. She also explains various obstetric manoeuvres such as induction, episiotomy and Caesarean section together with ways of avoiding or coping with them. *Offers informed guidance to enable the right choices to be made before, during and after the birth.*